I'd recommend this book to any pastor, especially those just starting in their ministry, and any others desiring to understand what faithful leadership in God's church looks like. Saturated in the gospel-depth that has characterized his other books, Jared Wilson shows us that a church leader is not just a defender of truth but a servant of people. I was particularly moved by Jared's challenge that we represent the love of God to people who walk through our doors. What an incredible and weighty privilege. May God use this book to raise up a generation of faithful servant leaders!

—J. D. Greear, pastor, the Summit Church,
president, Southern Baptist Convention

There are certain books that pastors should read once a year to regain their gospel sanity, clarity of calling, passion for the Savior, love for their people, and a renewed sense of what their daily work is. *Gospel-Driven Ministry* is one of those books. It holds the gospel forward not just as preachers' core message but also as the model and motivation for who pastors should be and what they are called to do. Pastors, buy this book and put it in your yearly reading rotation.

—Paul Tripp, pastor, speaker, author

Whether you are new pastor or a seasoned veteran of many years, *Gospel-Driven Ministry* will educate, instruct, and encourage you in your service to the Lord and his people. Combining personal experience, theological understanding, and a deep love for Christ's church, Jared Wilson offers timely wisdom for those called, in these challenging times, to shepherd the flock of God.

—Brian Brodersen, pastor, Calvary
Chapel, Costa Mesa, California

Current and future pastors—and those who love them—need to read this book. Jared Wilson opens up the pages of Scripture and his heart as well to give us the inside scoop on pastoral work and identity. Clearly he has a heart for ministry. With a quarter century of pastoral experience under his belt, he has much to share. Writing in a warm and personal style, Wilson explores most every aspect of ministry you can think of. Replete with scriptural references and personal examples, this is a volume of practical wisdom by which every pastor can chart a voyage through the tempestuous seas of contemporary ministry with confidence. Christ-centered and gospel-focused, this book is devoid of the platitudes and easy answers found in similar pastoral guides. Jared Wilson bares his soul in this book to share not only his profound insights into shepherding but also his anxieties, fears, and failures. In other words, he points not to himself but to Jesus, who is the great shepherd of the sheep and—thank God—of every pastor as well.

—HAROLD L. SENKBEIL, executive director emeritus, DOXOLOGY: The Lutheran Center for Spiritual Care and Counsel, author of *The Care of Souls*

Jared Wilson's new book, *Gospel-Driven Ministry*, represents my friend's steadfast commitment to marinate in the riches of God's grace, to steward both the wounds and joys of pastoral life, and to keep the gospel central to leaders and ministries. Jared writes with a depth beyond his years, wisdom gained after seminary, and a heart captured by the glory and grace of Jesus. Please give this book to neophytes and seasoned veterans in the ministry of the gospel.

—SCOTTY SMITH, pastor emeritus, Christ Community Church, Franklin, Tennessee, teacher in residence, West End Community Church, Nashville, Tennessee

*Gospel-Driven Ministry* is an honest, practical, instructive, and comprehensive work on pastoring that I wish would have been available to me twenty-five years ago. Jared writes from a rich and robust experience in ministry, sharing his pastoral highs with humility and his pastoral lows with vulnerability. This is a refreshing contribution to those setting out on the pastoral road and for those who might be weary walking it.

—J. R. VASSAR, lead pastor, Church at the Cross, Grapevine, Texas, author of *Glory Hunger*

Often in ministry things can be driven by pragmatics rather than principles. Rosters needs to be arranged, meetings attended, and sermons delivered. In the midst of the urgent, however, it is easy for the pastor to forget the very basis and purpose of their service. In *Gospel-Driven*

*Ministry* Jared Wilson provides a timely and necessary reminder of the transformative power of the *gospel* as the cornerstone of all effective pastoral ministry. With the warmth and wisdom of a seasoned pastor, Wilson calls the reader to consider not only the shape of their ministry but more importantly their motivation for it.

—Malcolm Gill, director of postgraduate studies, lecturer in Greek, New Testament, and homiletics, Sydney Missionary and Bible College, Sydney, Australia

Only an experienced pastor could write this book. It handles the vicissitudes of pastoral life and ministry with compassion. You'll feel known as you read it. But it is more than that. This book is treasure from a pastor who digs deeply when shepherding individual souls. It is wisdom for leading the whole church. If you apply its guidance, your flock will not only feel known but also be well-pastored. In fact, Jared Wilson's heart for Christ's church moved me to pastor better, and his pastoral gems showed me how to do so. Most importantly, absorbing this book will yield more of Christ in you and his church.

—Jonathan Dodson, lead pastor, City Life Church, and author of *Gospel-Centered Discipleship*, *Here in Spirit*, and *Our Good Crisis*

If you know one thing about Jared, it's that he has an unwavering passion for gospel-centrality. *Gospel-Driven Ministry* reads like a greatest hits of Jared's wisdom and experience from years of pastoring both local congregations and local pastors. A must-have for pastors and ministry leaders who desire to keep the gospel at the core of their ministry and practice.

—Ronnie Martin, lead pastor, Substance Church, Ashland, Ohio

Pastors, we are immersed in a consumeristic Christian culture where we have largely traded the biblical vision of pastoral ministry for executive leadership and organizational strategies. It's no surprise that many of us are confused and exhausted. In *Gospel-Driven Ministry*, Jared Wilson invites us to sit down and reimagine the call of pastor ministry in biblical terms, as a supernatural stewardship. You hold in your hands a book that will not only recalibrate your heart but will also reenergize your hands to navigate the practical day-to-day work among the people God has called you to serve. Again and again, Jared's writings set him apart as a true pastor to pastors. You will do well to apply his wise and experienced counsel.

—Matt Capps, senior pastor, Fairview Baptist
Church, Apex, North Carolina

We're in a pastoral ministry crisis. Evidence abounds—from pastors who are disqualifying themselves, to those who are burning out. Not to oversimplify matters, but I wonder if one reason for this crisis is a pastoral ministry that has become unmoored from the gospel. In *Gospel-Driven Ministry*, Jared Wilson, with clarity and the requisite pastoral experience, seeks to bring us back to the gospel roots that drive faithful pastoral ministry. If you are considering pastoral ministry or are in the habit of training gospel ministers, pick up this book and use it as a "gospel primer" for ministry. If you've been in ministry for some time and are doubting yourself or your ministry, struggling to press on, pick up this book as a "gospel refresher" for ministry. A ministry rooted in the good news of all that God is for us in Christ will magnify our triune God and encourage his people.

—Juan R. Sanchez, senior pastor, High Pointe
Baptist Church, Austin, Texas

# GOSPEL-DRIVEN MINISTRY

Jared C. Wilson

# GOSPEL
# DRIVEN
# MINISTRY

## An Introduction
## to the Calling and
## Work of a Pastor

ZONDERVAN
REFLECTIVE

ZONDERVAN REFLECTIVE

*Gospel-Driven Ministry*
Copyright © 2021 by Jared C. Wilson

Requests for information should be addressed to:
Zondervan, *3900 Sparks Dr. SE, Grand Rapids, Michigan 49546*

Zondervan titles may be purchased in bulk for educational, business, fundraising, or sales promotional use. For information, please email SpecialMarkets@Zondervan.com.

ISBN 978-0-310-11156-6 (hardcover)
ISBN 978-0-310-12022-3 (audio)
ISBN 978-0-310-11157-3 (ebook)

Published in association with Don Gates of the literary agency The Gates Group, www.the-gates-group.com.

*Cover design: Emily Weigel*
*Cover art: © Vanzyst/Shutterstock*
*Interior design: Denise Froehlich*

*Printed in the United States of America*

20 21 22 23 24  /LSC/  10 9 8 7 6 5 4 3 2 1

*For Nathan Rose*

# CONTENTS

# FOREWORD

A nd there was much weeping on the part of all" (Acts 20:37). This flood of tears poured out when the apostle Paul said farewell to the leaders of the Ephesian church and they said farewell to him. They didn't give him a gold watch. They broke down and wept—all of them together. A pastor's affection for his congregation, and their affection for him, can be that powerful, for the glory of Christ.

The more our world spirals down in poisonous rage, accusations, and ridicule, the more we pastors and our churches can shine. By his grace, we can embody the love of Christ together. Then we will stand out with public obviousness as islands of shalom in an ocean of toxins.

In a way, our world is already a loving place. Parents love their children, citizens love their countries, teenagers love their friends, and so forth. Good. What if none of this love existed at all, to soften and cheer human existence in this world? But all worldly love goes only so far (Matt 5:43-48). It is sincere but also fragile, delicate, touchy.

The love of Jesus endured the cross. And he calls pastors and churches into his love for the display of his glory. In fact, this is his simple but powerful strategy for our prophetic presence in this world: "As I have loved you, you must love one another. By this all people will know that you are my disciples, if you love for one another" (John 13:34-35). That beautiful command does not apply to some denominations only, it doesn't require a certain amount of any church's budget, it needs no law of protection from the state. Here in a world of rage, whoever we are, wherever we are, we Christians can embody the love of Christ.

That's where we pastors come in.

As Jared Wilson helps us see with practical clarity in this wonderful book, we pastors have been given a unique and sacred privilege. We are not salesmen pitching a product. We are not nags scolding the naughty children. We are not coaches keeping the team psyched up. Yes, we persuade and exhort and inspire. But above all else, we preach good news for bad people through the finished work of Christ on the cross and the endless power of the Holy Spirit. And this good news imparts *life*. It's why Jared boldly writes, "Pastors are in the business of bringing the dead to life through the power of God."

No wonder the divine strategy works! How can death defeat life? How can hatred cancel love? How can darkness conceal light? How can folly outsmart wisdom? Every other reality in this world is secondary, derivative, dependent—even parasitic. But the Son of God coming down into this world 2,000 years ago was the most original event since the creation. And the living Christ today is moving in all the nations, creating a community of life in a world of death— wherever we pastors bring his life-giving Word to exhausted, fed-up, desperate sinners.

Pastor, your ministry is an ongoing miracle. You're not making it happen. Jesus is. Let the wonder of that, the mystery of it, strengthen you for every pastoral task he gives you.

*Gospel-Driven Ministry: An Introduction to the Calling and Work of a Pastor* offers you a readable, thoughtful, seminary-level survey of both the wonder and the practice of pastoral ministry—in the wonder-working power of the gospel. If you are a veteran pastor, this book will serve you as a resource for mentoring younger pastors. If you are a new pastor, this book will be "orientation week" for your freshman year. If you are some years into your ministry, busier than you expected, buffeted by distractions, this book will help you realign with the commitments you must return to.

What you can expect from this book is a combination of biblical insight and practical wisdom. What you will *not* have to suffer through is hifalutin theory disconnected from real-life ministry, *nor* will you have to put up with handy-dandy tips disconnected from biblical authority and depth. Jared Wilson is a read-the-Bible man, and he is a get-the-job-done man. Does that resonate with you? So will this book.

Then, very soon, you will say farewell to your congregation. The Lord will call you away to another church, or he will call you home. In the meantime, if you receive the priorities and insights of this book with sincere tenderness of heart and gentle diligence in practice, then at your farewell, like Paul's so long ago, there will be much weeping on the part of all. And the watching world will be compelled to say, "Maybe Jesus really is the Prince of Peace."

Ray Ortlund
Pastor to Pastors
Immanuel Nashville

# ON THIS MYSTERIOUS STEWARDSHIP

> When you read this, you can perceive my insight into the mystery of Christ.
> **—EPHESIANS 3:4 ESV**

The gospel is the greatest power known to humankind because it alone can transform from death to life. Not even our brightest medical or technological minds can manage this feat. They are working on immortality, but they will fail. The Babel towers of human invincibility will all crumble; but this foolish message of a Judean carpenter crucified, buried, and dead will transform the whole world.

He conquered death. And you and I can, too, through the holy, spiritual power of the gospel.

That God would entrust this power to ordinary mortals like you and me is utterly astounding. As if only to further demonstrate the supernatural power of the foolish message of the cross, he gives it freely to fools to proclaim. We ponder a great mystery: ordinary sinners like you and like me are entrusted with the tending of Christ's little lambs. But, despite the daunting responsibility of this mind-boggling stewardship, we can persevere. Despite the pain and the trouble, we can persevere. Despite our slowness and our sin, we can persevere. Not because we are great shepherds, but because he is.

In 1 Timothy 3, Paul provides a discourse on the qualifications for church leaders. Elders must be like *this*, he says. Deacons must be like *that*. And then, as if vitally connected to this list of standards, he writes at the end of the passage:

Great indeed, we confess, is the mystery of godliness:

> He was manifested in the flesh,
> vindicated by the Spirit,
> seen by angels,
> proclaimed among the nations,
> believed on in the world,
> taken up in glory. (1 Tim 3:16 ESV)

There would seem to be a disconnect. Why a reference to the "mystery of godliness" and a rehearsal of gospel doctrine at the end of this biblical guide to church leadership? Because Paul knows that Christian ministry is pointless if it is not founded on, fueled by, and exulting in the grace of God given to us in Jesus, the Christ.

The simple gospel makes sense of the mystery of Christian ministry; indeed, the simple gospel *is* the mystery of Christian ministry. The most powerful message known to humankind—able to make sinners into saints and saints more like Jesus—has been entrusted to us. Pastors are in the business of bringing the dead to life through the power of God.

Paul commends this sacred stewardship over and over again.

The simple gospel can even be grasped by children. And yet the breadth of the mystery lies ever before us. None of us can span its greatness. Given a lifetime of Sundays to preach God's grace, we find we can barely scratch the surface.

We are privileged, by grace, to know Christ. And yet we do not yet know him as we will on that day. So, the mystery remains.

Of course, all Christians are called to know, enjoy, and center on the gospel. But the bar of maturity is set higher for pastors (1 Tim 3; Titus 1; 1 Peter 5). The accountability for pastors is also heightened (James 3:1; 1 Peter 5:3). And pastors share a unique responsibility for "keeping watch" over the Christians entrusted to them (Heb. 13:17). Thus, the call upon the lives of pastors to know and preach the gospel is more pronounced.

This book is about the ways in which those given the stewardship of this mystery—pastors of local churches—must meditate on it, proclaim it, and adorn it with their lives (and their deaths). By centering on the gospel, we are given the strength and joy to carry out this momentous task. In the thick of navigating the world of confused or cantankerous church members and hostile critics, preaching regularly to hard heads and hard hearts, holding the hands of those who are suffering, and rejoicing with the joyful, we increasingly see how far God's grace goes, both for us and for others. And we learn that other biblical mystery, the one akin to the strangeness of a holy God loving unholy men: it is a blessing to tend God's lambs. This book celebrates that mysterious blessing and guides pastors in the stewardship of it.

# CHAPTER 1

# THE PASTOR

The shepherd of God's people must bring his whole soul to the exercise of ministry. The minister must not envision the pastorate as merely the outlet for his academic inclinations. Nor is the pastorate purely about organizational leadership or, God forbid, entrepreneurial dream casting. It is a pouring out of one life for the sake of others. "I will most gladly spend and be spent for your souls," Paul tells the church at Corinth (2 Cor 12:15 ESV). Anything less is simply an engagement in religious machinery.

Of course, the increasing social and technological complexity of each successive age has brought to the church in the West an ever-increasing ministerial and occupational complexity that our predecessors in the faith could not foresee. Frequently, this complexity affords the traditional pastor fewer churches amenable to his ministry and sometimes little appreciation when he does find one. Ministers today are expected to be gifted public speakers and catalytic leaders, yet very little else. The CEO model of ministry dominates, even in normal-sized churches. Whatever "pasture work" is deemed necessary can be outsourced.

Sometimes, I peruse the ministerial want ads online and wonder,

"Does anyone even know what a pastor is anymore?" For instance, a Colorado church recently used a church staffing website to advertise its need for a pastor who would be willing to repreach the sermons of famous preachers word for word in exchange for ninety percent of the tithes and offerings. "We have everything needed for the church," the ad read, "except the pastor." As a consumeristic ethos swallows religion whole, what every church apparently needs is just a performance artist treating the church like a sales job.

The extremity of this example does not overshadow the more mundane reality of consumerism in the churches down the street or in your own church. I routinely hear from church planters struggling under the weight of attendance expectations and growth projections from their sponsoring associations, denominational officers, and donors. They want to feed the sheep, but the people who hold the purse strings want them rallying goats. The pastoral heart strains.

Do we know what it means to be a pastor? In order to be fueled by the gospel rather than the world, we must look to Scripture to define what a pastor is, outline the pastoral job description, and determine which candidates are eligible for the job.

## What Is a Pastor?

The most common word found in the New Testament for the office or position of pastor is the word *elder*. The book of Acts details the establishment and growth of the Christian church after Jesus's ascension and the outpouring of the Holy Spirit on the day of Pentecost. In this historical narrative of Christianity's missionary expansion, we see how the apostles led the planting of local churches, the first congregational communities of the burgeoning church of Jesus Christ. In Acts 14:23, for instance, we see that the apostles established elders in every church. And the continuing pattern throughout the New Testament is that there were a plurality of elders in each local congregation.

In many translations of the Bible, the word *elder* (from the Greek *presbuteros*) is used interchangeably with the verbiage around *pastor* and the office labeled as *overseer*. Mark Dever writes:

> Acts 20:17–38 shows that the words *elders* (*presbuterous*, v. 17) and *overseers* (*episkopous*, v. 28 [also known as bishops]) are interchangeable, and that both do the work of pastoring (*poimainein*, v. 28) or shepherding God's flock. A pastor, then, is an elder, and an elder is a bishop/overseer—all three terms refer to the same office and the same work of pastoring.[1]

Although modern use of titles sometimes distinguishes the offices, biblically speaking, pastors are elders and elders are pastors.

## What Does a Pastor Do?

We see the first indication of the pastor's special task at the establishing of the diaconate in Acts 6. In order to facilitate more effective ministry within the church, the apostles have the church select seven men to practically address the neglect of Greek widows in the church's benevolence ministry. The primary distinction revealed in this passage is that the apostles (and their pastoral successors) are responsible for "prayer and the ministry of the word" (6:4)—the spiritual life of the church—and deacons are responsible for "serving tables" (6:2)—the physical caretaking and service that sustains the practical life of the church.

In Ephesians 4:11–12, Paul writes that pastors are one of several key roles given to the church by God to "equip the saints for the work of ministry" (ESV).

Thus, pastors are the church leaders responsible for the theological vision, ministerial training, and spiritual discipleship of

---

1. Mark Dever and Paul Alexander, *The Deliberate Church: Building Your Ministry on the Gospel* (Wheaton, IL: Crossway, 2005), 132.

the congregation. Tasks under these headings as reflected in the Scriptures include (but are not limited to):

- Studying the Scriptures and preaching/teaching (1 Tim 3:2; Titus 1:9)
- Spiritual counseling and other kinds of pastoral care (Acts 20:28; 2 Cor 1:3–4)
- Laying hands on and praying for the sick (James 5:14)
- Setting examples for the church in godly living (1 Tim 5:3)
- Protecting the church from false teaching (Titus 1:9–11)
- Prayerfully setting vision for the church's mission (1 Peter 5:2)
- Leading the exercise of church discipline (Matt 18:17; 1 Tim 5:19–20)
- Providing accountability for other elders; collectively exercising authority over a lead pastor or teacher (1 Tim 5:17; Acts 15:6)
- Developing future leaders and other teachers (1 Tim 4:14)

Admittedly, there is some overlap between pastoral ministry and diaconal ministry. In fact, the biblical qualifications for each office are curiously similar, although 1 Timothy 3:1–13 reveals that elders are additionally required to be "able to teach."

There will frequently be overlap of the spiritual and the practical,[2] and of course, in the Christian life, everything should be considered spiritual. The spiritual work of the elders should not be considered impractical or merely intellectual, and the practical work of the deacons should not be considered unspiritual or merely pragmatic. Likewise, the leadership of elders should not be viewed as *not*

---

2. One example of an area of overlap is the visitation of orphans, widows, shut-ins, or the ill. These souls often require both physical/practical care and spiritual guidance, counseling, and encouragement in the Word. On a case-by-case basis, this work can be the responsibility of only elders, only deacons, or both elders and deacons working together.

*service*, and the service of deacons should not be seen as *not leadership*. Nevertheless, the division of labor is between authoritative leadership and assisting servanthood. To put it another way, elders serve by leading and deacons lead by serving. And *the primary way pastors serve by leading is by proclaiming the Word of God and by setting an example in godly living*.

## Who May Be a Pastor?

Now that we have established what a pastor is and what a pastor does, we must determine who may be one. We will see that qualified Christian men who are called by God and commissioned by others are God's choice for the job.

### Qualified

The qualifications for elders can be found most directly in 1 Timothy 3:1–7, Titus 1:5–9, and 1 Peter 5:1–3. As we consider the composite portrait resulting from each passage, we might chart the qualifications this way:

| 1 Timothy 3:1–7 | Titus 1:5–9 | 1 Peter 5:1–3 |
|---|---|---|
| above reproach | blameless, upright, holy | |
| faithful to his wife | faithful to his wife | |
| temperate | not quick-tempered | |
| self-controlled | self-controlled, disciplined | |
| respectable | loves what is good | |
| hospitable | hospitable | |
| able to teach | instruct in sound doctrine | |
| not given to drunkenness | not given to drunkenness | |

| 1 Timothy 3:1–7 | Titus 1:5–9 | 1 Peter 5:1–3 |
|---|---|---|
| not violent but gentle | not violent | not lording it over others |
| not quarrelsome | not overbearing | |
| not a lover of money | not pursuing dishonest gain | not pursuing dishonest gain |
| manage family well | children believe and are not wild or disobedient | |
| not a recent convert | | |
| good reputation | | |
| | holds firmly to trustworthy message | |
| | | willing |

The most extensive list of qualifications comes in 1 Timothy 3; Titus 1 offers a similar list with only minor alterations; and 1 Peter 5 repeats a couple and makes a new contribution. We must take these passages in composite to understand who may be a pastor. These passages together allow us to construct a list of qualifications for the office of elder:

- Faithful husbands (if they are married) or chaste (if they are not)
- Fathers to children raised in the Lord (if they have children)
- Reasonable, calm, "long-tempered"
- Self-controlled, self-disciplined, and gentle
- Respected and blameless before others
- Able to teach and preach (this is essentially what sets the pastoral office apart from the diaconate, though there's something else I'll review shortly, as well)
- Knowledgeable in doctrine
- Willing to correct and rebuke violations of doctrine
- Hospitable

Pastors should not be:

- Greedy
- Arrogant
- Short-tempered or contentious
- Addicted to drug or drink
- A recent convert to the faith

Please note what is *not* on the list of qualifications. The apostles Paul and Peter say nothing about leadership skills per se, nothing about creativity, nothing about personality types or entrepreneurial giftedness. With one exception, the pastoral qualifications are about character, disposition, and spiritual maturity—and they set the bar very high. The only qualification that could be interpreted as a skill is "able to teach," a distinguishing mark between the pastorate and the diaconate.

But there's something else that distinguishes the pastoral office, which is that qualified pastors are to be qualified *men*. The roles of women in the New Testament church were diverse and vital to the mission of the gospel. Women served, led, and taught in a variety of ways in the early congregations—think of Priscilla's influence on Apollos, for instance (Acts 18:24–28)—just as they ought to today. Women are just as integral as men to the life of the body. However, following from the biblical teaching on male headship in the home and church (Eph 5:22–33; Col 3:18–19), Paul's most clear teaching— and of course most controversial teaching—on the roles of men and women in the governance of the church restricts the pastorate to men. In 1 Timothy 2:11–14, he writes: "Let a woman learn quietly with all submissiveness. I do not permit a woman to teach or to exer- cise authority over a man; rather, she is to remain quiet. For Adam was formed first, then Eve; and Adam was not deceived, but the woman was deceived and became a transgressor" (ESV). This short passage is a complicated one, and this space cannot be dedicated to a thorough analysis of the biblical teaching on women's roles in the church. Broadly speaking, as it pertains to church leadership roles, *egalitarianism* is the view that holds that the office of pastor is open to both qualified men and women. Egalitarians offer different interpretations of 1 Timothy 2:11–14, but the most frequent one perhaps argues that Paul is referring to a specific discipline situation in a local church and is not issuing a binding stricture for every church in every age. *Complementarianism* is the view that argues that while women are equal to men in worth and dignity, they are excluded from the pastoral office. Most complementarians would say that because Paul is grounding his stricture in the creation order, he is not simply speaking to a specific circumstance but also offering a binding stricture for every church in every age.

There are, of course, a variety of shades and nuances within each of the two major viewpoints that often necessitate whole books to hash out. I cannot do the intricacies of the ongoing debate justice here. But the viewpoint represented in this book rests on what is taken as the plainest point, which is that the office of pastor is reserved only for men. What Paul affirms is male headship/authority in the church, and the teaching that is in accordance with that. And Paul roots his declaration in the creation order, making it a foundational guideline not a cultural one.

Throughout the Scriptures, we see only men in positions of authority over the people of God, from the priests in the old covenant to the overseers in the new. Jesus's twelve disciples were all male, despite the apparent constant presence of females among his followers. When the qualifications of elders and deacons in the church are listed in the New Testament, only the office of deacon comes with a corresponding list of female qualifications, indicating not a list of requirements for deacons' wives (as commonly translated) but rather a list of requirements for female deacons. This difference indicates that women may serve in the office of deacon but not in the office of elder.

It is also notable that Paul connects the teaching on male headship in the church to the teaching ministry of the church. Again, he is distinguishing the pastorate from the diaconate with reference to the ministry of the Word. Deacons may be male or female and teaching ability is not among their qualifications; elders must be qualified males because their role is defined by authoritative teaching.

These qualifications are what makes for a biblically qualified pastor. A man may be creative, entrepreneurial, theologically excellent, a real "people person," a born orator, and a visionary leader; but if he is not qualified according to the apostolic record, he shouldn't be a pastor.

## Called

What is a call to ministry?

A call to pastoral ministry is the inclination to conform one's desires and direction to the aspiration of shepherding a church. It must not simply be a desire to preach. Preaching is a part of pastoring, but it is not the entirety of it. It must not simply be a desire to lead. Lots of people desire to lead others but should not be overseeing a congregation.

Nearly every specific call directed to an individual for a particular ministry depicted in the Scriptures is a distinctly supernatural thing. Audible voices are manifest throughout the Old Testament call narratives. In the New Testament, we see Paul meeting Christ on the road to Damascus or, in Acts 16, seeing the vision of the Macedonian man calling for help. Very few—if any—of us will have such experiences today. I don't know why; we just don't.

And, yet, the call to pastoral ministry today is no less supernatural. It may be less dramatic today, but the Spirit's calling of a man to overseeing a church is still a miracle. That the Lord would continue to draw sinners into this special stewardship of the gospel is a great mercy. And a great mystery! But how does it work?

It is customary for pastoral aspirants to speak of "feeling called."

And I don't believe there is anything inherently wrong with that. There are, for pastors, essentially two components of calling—an internal call and an external call.

The internal call, the inclination toward ministry that appears to "come out of nowhere" and strike one as the right path to pursue, is a subjective experience of God's will that might arise from one's commitment to the local church, the practice of spiritual disciplines, or simply the consideration of ministerial interests and personal passions. For some, the internal call is more dramatic than that. It is not an inclination so much as a kind of revelation. There is no audible voice or beaming light from heaven, but a distinct Spiritual notion that was not there before is suddenly manifest.

I believe the Lord called me to vocational ministry the week of youth camp the summer between my seventh and eighth grade years. It was an early morning, and I sat at a picnic table conducting my morning devotions. I was mainly trying to impress a girl. Reading in Exodus 3 of God's call to Moses through the burning bush, I found the text resonating with me in a way it never had before.

Moses played up his insecurities. So did I. Moses had a speech impediment. So did I. Moses did not aspire to ministry prior to this call. Neither did I.

I did not come from a ministry family. We were churchgoers, and my parents were genuine believers, but there was no legacy of pastoral ministry in my life to which I felt obliged to contribute. Nobody had ever suggested to me I ought to think about vocational ministry. I could not recollect ever giving it a second's thought until that morning, when I believed that the Lord was unmistakably telling me what he wanted me to be when I grew up. While this idea originated outside myself as a prompting or leading from the Lord, the experience was personal and specific, subjective to my own interpretation. I *felt* called. This is an example of an internal call.

An external call is when one actually experiences a church or church leader pointing out one's aptitude or potential fitness for ministry. When someone in ministerial authority encourages you by saying, "You should follow a course toward ministry. We need you. We can use you. You should do this," that is an external call.

Perhaps the idea has not ever crossed the prospective minister's mind, but it has now been placed there by an outside influence. And yet, the external call should correspond to an internal call, and vice versa. Why? Because no pastor should be thrust into his position under any kind of duress or full of reluctance (external call without internal), nor should anyone pursue pastoral ministry as a lone wolf without the support and counsel of other elders and leaders in the broader body of Christ (internal call without external). Remember, in 1 Peter 5:2, Peter says to shepherd "not under compulsion, but willingly . . . eagerly" (ESV). In 1 Timothy 3:1, Paul encourages one who "aspires" to oversee God's flock.

In one of my pastorates, I had begun the task of leading the church to move away from the solo pastor model and to appoint a plurality of elders. As I assessed potential elder candidates, I invariably came across men who expressed a sense of their own unworthiness for the office and intimidation about the role. I certainly appreciated their humility! I would worry more about a pastor who never felt intimidated by the role and who always thought, "Of course I should be a pastor!" That can indicate the kind of arrogance the Bible forbids.

And yet, humility is one thing, and self-pity or reluctance is another. I appreciate the self-deprecation of one who feels unworthy of the task, but I would also be loathe to install any elder who did not feel a sense of honor, excitement, and personal desire for it.

The external call is not enough. No one should become a pastor because somebody else twisted their arm or patted them on the back. They should aspire to it humbly and also be responding in some sense to an internal call.

What the call is primarily aimed at is *not* a title, nor even an office in the church, but a qualification of the heart! In other words, you don't have to be qualified (yet) for ministry to be called to it; but, in such cases, the call to ministry should be taken as a call to pursue qualification for that ministry. This is really important, because sometimes Christians are prone to saying things like, "God doesn't call the qualified, he qualifies the called." This is a half-truth, insofar as God very often calls the qualified; however, when he calls the unqualified, he really does mean for them to become qualified *before* they assume responsibility for a congregation. To put it in obviously silly terms, if my call at seventh grade was genuine, that did not mean I was immediately qualified to begin pastoring a church. And the same would be true if it had happened when I was forty years old. *A call alone is not permission for the pastorate.*

We see this strange dynamic play out in some of the more high-profile cases of fallen pastors looking for restoration to ministry. They sometimes quote Romans 11:29—"for God's gifts and his call are irrevocable"—which is a gross misinterpretation of the text because it's not about a subjective call to ministry but the objective call of God to salvation. The idea at work among these disqualified men is that a sense of calling trumps everything. This is unbiblical and dangerous.

Calling does not replace qualification. The call to ministry, then, is a call to become qualified or a call to maintain one's qualifications. This is why fallen pastors must start at the place of the new convert. There can be no immediate restoration to the office of minister. To the fellowship? Yes, granted that they have repented. But to the pastorate? They must put in as much time as it takes to restore their ability to stand under the qualifications listed in 1 Timothy 3, Titus 1, and 1 Peter 5.

A call to pastoral ministry is the inclination to conform one's desires and direction to the aspiration of shepherding a church. That this calling is subjective does not mean it is unimportant. A call to ministry is vital for pastors, whether they are vocational elders or lay elders. But one reason we have to maintain the subjectivity of an individual call is that we run the danger of treating a call as superior to qualifications or to the confirmation of others, an error to which we now turn our discussion.

## Commissioned

We have a strange movement of ministerial freelancing that takes place in the West, and it is driven a lot by the way we "do church." In most respects, it works out when a church puts together a pastoral search team, places an ad, and then interviews and assesses applicants. But that's not how the New Testament church found its pastors.

In Acts, the apostles appointed elders from among the people to authoritatively shepherd the people (14:23). The qualifications in Titus 1 are, in fact, placed in a similar circumstantial context. In verse 5, Paul is telling Titus to establish elders. The qualifications Paul lists are his way of telling Titus what to look for in potential candidates.

If you go all the way back to Exodus 18, you can see the genesis of the practices of appointing a plurality of elders.

> The next day Moses took his seat to serve as judge for the people, and they stood around him from morning till evening. When his father-in-law saw all that Moses was doing for the people, he said, "What is this you are doing for the people? Why do you alone sit as judge, while all these people stand around you from morning till evening?"
>
> Moses answered him, "Because the people come to me to seek God's will. Whenever they have a dispute, it is brought to me, and I decide between the parties and inform them of God's decrees and instructions."
>
> Moses' father-in-law replied, "What you are doing is not good. You and these people who come to you will only wear yourselves

out. The work is too heavy for you; you cannot handle it alone. Listen now to me and I will give you some advice, and may God be with you. You must be the people's representative before God and bring their disputes to him. Teach them his decrees and instructions, and show them the way they are to live and how they are to behave. But select capable men from all the people—men who fear God, trustworthy men who hate dishonest gain—and appoint them as officials over thousands, hundreds, fifties and tens. Have them serve as judges for the people at all times, but have them bring every difficult case to you; the simple cases they can decide themselves. That will make your load lighter, because they will share it with you. If you do this and God so commands, you will be able to stand the strain, and all these people will go home satisfied."

Moses listened to his father-in-law and did everything he said. He chose capable men from all Israel and made them leaders of the people, officials over thousands, hundreds, fifties and tens. They served as judges for the people at all times. The difficult cases they brought to Moses, but the simple ones they decided themselves. (Exod 18:13–26)

Moses is told to "select capable men from the people." You see the beginning of the qualifications for godly leadership in this passage: "hate dishonest gain" and "trustworthy" reminds us of Paul saying to Titus, "He must hold firm to the trustworthy word as taught" (1:9 ESV). Jethro doesn't suggest Moses collect resumes. No, he wants him to find those from within the people who have good reputations and are godly. This is the normative and most advantageous means of finding a pastor.

But even if a pastor is coming to a new church to lead, he should be the product of a church that has confirmed his qualifications. Think of Paul laying hands on Timothy (1 Tim 4:14). There is an ecclesial commissioning, a "stamp of approval" that serves as a sign from the congregation of its conviction that a person is qualified. By commissioning, I mean a confirmation of pastoral qualifications by a congregation or congregational representation. As Jason K. Allen has said, "You don't select the church; the church selects you."[3]

The pastoral office is undeniably connected to a local congregation. It is certainly appropriate to sometimes speak of "pastoring" as a kind of ministry that can be conducted outside a church context (military and hospital chaplains do pastoral work, campus ministers do pastoral work, etc.), but the role of pastor is inextricably connected to a particular people for whom and to whom the pastor is covenantally responsible. Only a church submissively recognizing a spiritual leader grants that person the title "Pastor"—a seminary degree or an ordination certificate alone does not.

In the Southern Baptist tradition, churches have historically broken down the process of commissioning pastors into two categories: licensing and ordination. Very few churches still conduct ministry licensing, and it is reserved most often today for legal clearance in certain states for officiating religious ceremonies. But in the past, it was reserved as a kind of "prequalification" for a young man who has shown gifts to preach and evidence of a call to ministry. The "ministry license" was a formal way to declare him essentially qualified for eldership without his holding the office. In the days of my youth, being licensed typically meant you were free to "marry 'em and bury 'em." Licensing was the first step for a young pastoral candidate, usually occurring before or during his undergraduate years, with ordination typically withheld until his completion of a seminary degree.

This is a fine tradition when carried out with circumspection, but there are two significant weaknesses when it isn't: First, it equates a seminary education with a qualification to pastor. I say this as a seminary professor myself, but it is possible to get a stellar theological education and still not be qualified to pastor. Now, hopefully, your pursuit of academic training has not just equipped you to be

---

3. Jason K. Allen, *Discerning Your Call to Ministry: How to Know for Sure and What to Do about It* (Chicago: Moody Publishers, 2016), 74.

"able to teach," but also shaped your character and aided you in your pursuit of holiness and the cultivation of the fruit of the Spirit in your life. But in the end, an academic institution cannot be the real judge of that. Only a church can.

Secondly, it places the substantial formation of the pastor on an educational institution rather than the church herself. Evangelicalism is overrun today with men who hold seminary degrees but not much pastoral sensibility. Many of these men have spurned church formation and ignored church commissioning.

Some aspiring pastors receive no vetting anywhere. They have no real church home, no mentorship, no training, no discipling. They've been equipped wholly by books and podcasts and social media; they skip formal education and go plant a church like one might start a lemonade stand.

Such cases are extreme, but the bottom line is this: _someone who wants to serve over a church should be a product of a church._ Even if your process doesn't resemble the traditional ordination pathway, there should be a way of receiving a stamp of approval from the flock that has produced you.

The pastorate is not a right or an entitlement. The pastorate is a sacred stewardship reserved only for qualified, called, and commissioned men. We set ourselves up for failure at all that matters when we try to circumvent the biblical guidelines for pastoral ministry. But the recovery of this high bar will have nothing but positive effects on the church as a whole and her advancement of gospel mission.

## For Reflection

1. Describe your own sense of calling to the work of ministry. Have you experienced both an internal and an external call? Explain.
2. As you survey the list of qualifications for the pastorate, where do you think you are strongest? Weakest?

3. What is your plan to develop in your areas of weakness?

4. Whether you are currently in vocational ministry or not, in what ways are you currently demonstrating a shepherd's love for his flock?

5. How does the gospel inform your ongoing pursuit of the biblical qualifications for ministry?

## For Further Study:

Bridges, Charles. *The Christian Ministry.* Carlisle, PA: Banner of Truth, 1959.

> This classic work from the early nineteenth-century English vicar is breathtaking in its exhaustive treatment of the ministerial office and pastoral tasks. Nearly two hundred years since its first printing, it is still largely unrivaled.

Gregory the Great, Saint. *The Book of Pastoral Rule.* Translated by George E. Demacopoulos. New York: St Vladimir's Seminary Press, 2007.

> This thorough examination of pastoral ministry from the patristic era is one of the church's earliest works on the subject. It is not without its challenges for Protestant readers in the modern era, but it is a rewarding read.

Spurgeon, Charles Haddon. *Lectures to My Students.* Carlisle, PA: Banner of Truth, 2008.

> Perhaps still the gold standard for a complete ministerial education in literary form, this work from the Victorian era's Prince of Preachers spends much of its time on homiletics but still offers invaluable insights for the pastor's character and disciplines.

# CHAPTER 2

# THE POWER

She sat on the edge of her seat, both nervous and eager. As she chewed on her lip and wrung her hands, I could tell she had a lot to say.

I sat to the side of my desk, trying to appear relaxed, speaking pleasantly, my hands folded gently in my lap. I had announced my resignation from this pastorate not long before and had spent my remaining weeks entertaining a litany of "parting thoughts" from my soon-to-be-former flock. This woman had some things to get off her chest.

So, she proceeded to air all her grievances. Some were things I'd heard here and there before, mainly things I couldn't really do anything to change—my particular theological views, for instance. Some were things I was hearing for the first time. Some were things I've now spent years considering in the rearview mirror and still consider to be invented out of whole cloth. But I sat and listened without judgment. I wanted to honor her even if she wasn't returning the favor. To be a pastor often means to subject one's self to the weaponized disappointments of others. Rather than defend myself, rather than debate, I just decided to take the hits.

And then, she said the absolute worst thing I could have heard in that moment:

"We know, Jared," she said, "that the gospel is your thing . . ."

The sentiment starts out great. Indeed, I am overjoyed to be thought of as the pastor whose "thing" is the gospel. But it was just a setup for a calamity:

". . . but sometimes," she continued, "we need to hear other things."

My heart sank.

For years, I had not only explicated the good news of Jesus Christ from God's breathed-out Word, I had been making the case for the thorough-going-ness of the gospel, the need for grace in all of life—for the saved and the unsaved—from the same Word. Somehow, she either hadn't heard or didn't believe. "Yeah, yeah, of course gospel," she seemed to be saying, "but what else you got?"

Crushed, I thanked her for sharing her heart with me and resolved to pray for her, despite my hurts. Of all the complaints lodged against my philosophy, my personality, my leadership decisions, the most disheartening thing she could have said was that she thought the gospel was simply not enough. She wanted more.

This is not simply a theological disagreement. It is a deficiency of the heart and of the soul. In fact, if this woman could be diagnosed with a kind of gospel amnesia, the prescription would be the exact opposite of her request—not less gospel but more! "The solution to our deadness to God's grace," as Ray Ortlund says, "is more grace."

The pastor's business is souls. And to get at a soul, one must have real power. One must have power beyond inspiration or emotional uplift. Minds may be informed by TED talks. Hearts may be touched by Hallmark movies. But the soul can only be changed by supernatural power. And *there is only one place the pastor can find supernatural power—the Spirit of God working through the message of the gospel, the finished work of the Son of God.*

Shepherds of the flock are called primarily to the gospel—to

believe it, to dwell in it, and to proclaim it. The prophet Isaiah pro-
claims the vision for this proclamation at a turning point in the
covenantal history of God's people:

> Go on up to a high mountain,
> > O Zion, herald of good news;
> lift up your voice with strength,
> > O Jerusalem, herald of good news;
> > lift it up, fear not;
> say to the cities of Judah,
> > "Behold your God!"
> Behold, the Lord GOD comes with might,
> > and his arm rules for him;
> behold, his reward is with him,
> > and his recompense before him.
> He will tend his flock like a shepherd;
> > he will gather the lambs in his arms;
> he will carry them in his bosom,
> > and gently lead those that are with young. (Isa 40:9–
> > > 11 ESV)

Where does Isaiah get this burden for the priority of the good news?
We might look back to his sixth chapter, where he beholds the glory
of the LORD in the temple. The train of the LORD's majesty fills the
place. Isaiah is overcome, undone, spiritually discombobulated. And
then he is, in a sense, put back together—but never the same. The
awe of this experience immediately fuels his missional availability.
Because he has tasted and seen that the LORD is good, he is willing
to go anywhere and do anything to get this vision of glory out of the
temple and into the world.

But the ministry to which God calls Isaiah is fearsome. The LORD
promises him that he will encounter hard-hearted people. He will
suffer reviling and rejection. He will be persecuted and profaned.

This ministry of suffering must continue, the LORD says, until he has, in fact, *lost* ninety percent of the people and only a faithful ten percent remain. The prophet is to keep on prophesying until the whole place feels forsaken and he himself feels forgotten, until whatever fruitfulness appeared to be there before becomes nothing but a stump.

Many pastors enduring difficult ministries of decline may resonate with this. Isaiah's ministry is not anything you and I would want for ourselves. But he had beheld just enough glory to become spiritually useful in any capacity God preferred. And at that point, God preferred an uphill slog against degeneracy and unrepentance.

But then we come to Isaiah 40, and there is a turn. If the Bible were an hourglass, Isaiah 40 would be the middle where the sands of time falling through the old covenant begin to accumulate and take shape to forecast the new age to come through Christ. Despite all the difficulty, no matter the trial, regardless of the pushback, the ministerial dictate begins like this: "Comfort my people. . . . Speak tenderly . . ." (Isa 40:1–2). But don't they need a good upbraiding, a stern scolding? Yet the LORD commands the proclamation of comfort.

With what should we comfort God's people, brothers? What should we speak to them? What words do we have? What message? In a world of religious noise, with so much competing for our attention; in a church culture that offers countless steps and tips and helpful hints; and amid a million ways to pull ourselves up by our bootstraps—what is the biblical shepherd actually called to do?

Cry out to the people, "Behold your God!"

This is what works! *Nothing else works to transform the soul. Only the glory of God.* When people come into your buildings on the weekends, when they come into your office for counseling, when they sit across the table from you for mentoring or discipling, what do you want them to see? What is it that will till up the hard soil in their hearts, that will lift up their gaze and fill their lungs with air? The answer is *not* your good advice. Your basic ministerial task in every context is to say to people both near and far from the Lord, "Behold your God!"

## The Glorious Gospel Is the Pastor's Central Message

In Isaiah 40:3–4 we are told that the crooked ways will be made straight, the low places made high, and the high places made low. This is an earth-shattering, world-shifting message. So why on earth, in some of our churches, would we save this message for special occasions?

True pastoral ministry does not begin with leadership skills or strategies, but with gospel exultation. It begins with worship. You've been taken apart by the glory of Christ and put back together by the glory of Christ, and you want to have nothing to do with ministry that has nothing to do with the glory of Christ. *The gospel is our central message.*

This makes absolute sense to those who've become so overwhelmed with the glory of Christ and so fixated on the wondrous story of his sinless life, sacrificial death, and powerful resurrection that they wouldn't spend time on anything else. They couldn't keep this glory to themselves. For others, it seems remedial, assumptive. But, pastor, everything your people need is bound up in the person and work of Jesus Christ alone.

> Behold, the Lord GOD comes with might,
>> and his arm rules for him;
> behold, his reward is with him,
>> and his recompense before him. (Isa 40:10 ESV)

This is what we need! Real power. Real strength. When that same married couple is sitting across from you rehearsing the same bitterness and resentments, and for the umpteenth time you are racking your brain for some marriage tip or something you read in a relationships book, and you're coming up empty, you may be tempted to forget that it is their souls for which you actually have a word.

I remember one young couple in particular sitting across from me in my study. The wife had reached out for marriage counseling. Seeking to clear the air after getting the general sense of her concern, I asked her to be as practical as she could about what her husband could do to show he loved her. She said, "I know he's exhausted when he comes home from work, but I'm exhausted too. What I would love is for him to take the kids into the living room and play with them so I can prepare dinner and wash the dishes without having them hanging all over me."

It sounds reasonable, doesn't it? She wasn't asking for more leisure time necessarily. She simply wanted to carry out her evening duties unencumbered. She wanted her children's father to take them off her hands for a bit.

I looked at the young husband for his response to this request. And do you want to know what this man said? He said, "Do you have a book that I can read?"

I said, "A book? You don't need a book. Your book is sitting right next to you. She just said what she'd like you to do. I heard it. You heard it, and not for the first time. Son, you know what to do. You just don't want to do it. Your problem is not a lack of information but a lack of heart."

And this is true of nearly all of us. Most times, our problem is not a lack of information on how to love God and love others. What we lack is the heart to do it. What we lack is power. The true love language of humanity is, in fact, the power of God. And this only comes to us through the good news of the finished work of Christ. The Holy Spirit working through the gospel is the only power given to us.

We see over and over again in the Scriptures not a graduating from the gospel, an "of course" presumption of the gospel or a "what else you got?" boredom with the gospel; rather, its pages direct us ever toward a wholehearted commitment to the centrality of the gospel and its glory as our only resource for the enduring work of ministry. Paul tells the Corinthians that he has resolved to "know nothing" among them except the message of Christ crucified (1 Cor 2:2). And then, later, he tells them that he shared the gospel as being "of first importance" (1 Cor 15:3–4), and I take him not to mean simply of *initial* importance but of utmost, central importance. He says to the Philippians, "Only let us hold true to what we have attained" (3:16 ESV). Previously he has expressed to them his ongoing desire to lay hold of the one who has laid hold of him (3:12).

The very shape of Paul's letters to the churches, in fact, details the central power of the gospel, as the apostle always begins with some kind of exposition of the finished work of Christ. The length of the exposition is usually scaled to the length of the letter, of course, but every letter begins with the indicative narrative of the gospel, from which all the practical matters—the imperatives of obedience and witness—then flow. This very compositional contour shows us the well from which Paul is drawing his power. It cannot be found in the law of obedience.

In 2 Corinthians 3, in fact, Paul compares and contrasts law and gospel, and after holding up the law as a glorious reflection of the perfect holiness of God, he nevertheless says that the gospel far exceeds it in glory (3:7–11). The ministry of the gospel "surpasses" the ministry of the law. And therein lies a rather provocative claim. Paul categorizes the gospel as "the ministry of righteousness," which is interesting, because we might normally assign that label to the law, which does, after all, reveal and prescribe righteousness. But Paul categorizes the law instead as "the ministry of condemnation."

Is this what you want your pastoral ministry to be? A rehearsal of condemnation?

You will say no, of course. And yet if you are preaching and discipling toward a steady diet of moralistic, "how to" messages, you are accomplishing exactly that. It may not look or sound like the hellfire and brimstone fundamentalism festering in the caricatures of legalism you've rejected, but positive and informal law is no less law than the negative and formal. "Do" is just a flip of the law coin from "Don't." The essential message of Christianity is, actually, "Done."

Thus, a regular preaching of practical application, moral inspiration, and religious do-goodism—detached from the central and empowering reality of the finished work of Christ—is a subtle and seductive means of leading people into condemnation. The law cannot change a heart, except perhaps to crush it.

Your central job as a pastor, then, is to center on the gospel. As Martin Luther says, ministers must "know this article well, teach it unto others, and beat it into their heads continually."[1] Keep pointing people to Jesus. You have very little business doing otherwise.

And there's so much there! The central gospel really is glorious. This was the chief source of my heartbreak with the woman's gospel amnesia in my office. She was somehow tired of hearing the astounding news that in her sins (and her works!) she stands condemned, but that God, out of his great love, sent his only Son to take her place, to take her punishment, to die her death, and then to become her resurrection. I know it is the "old, old story," but how can it get old to those who worship Christ? We will be rehearsing the gospel for all eternity (Rev 5:12). How on earth could it be boring?

Compared to Jesus, you are boring. Your good ideas are boring. Your creativity is boring. But the gospel cannot be boring. It is glorious, as it announces a multitude of blessings and riches in and through the person of Christ Jesus—forgiveness of sins, the imputation of his righteousness, spiritual union with him, adoption into his family as his brothers and sisters, reconciliation with the Father, and indwelling by the Spirit. From the facets of the atonement to the gifts and fruit of the Spirit, the gospel gleams with celestial beauty that cannot be outshined by the best eloquence or erudition. As

---

1. Martin Luther, *A Commentary on St. Paul's Epistle to the Galatians* (London: Smith, English, 1860), 206.

the old hymn "Great Is Thy Faithfulness" celebrates, in the gospel there is "strength for today and bright hope for tomorrow; blessings all mine and ten thousand beside!"

So, resolve like Paul to "know nothing" except the glorious gospel. It will preach. You will not run out of material. You and your people need it every single day; you couldn't wear it out in a lifetime of Sundays.

To be driven by the gospel's power for ministry necessitates centering on the gospel's power for your ministry. And this, of course, has enormous implications for the conducting of pastoral ministry, from our preaching on down.

## Gospel-Centrality Defines the Bible

If the gospel is the only power entrusted to us, it stands to reason that we would see this dynamic throughout all of Scripture. Perhaps you are still under the popular misconception that the Old Testament reflects a time when God related to his people by works, and the New Testament announces that God now relates by grace. But the law/gospel dynamic found in the New Testament runs throughout the entire Bible, even if expressions of it differ and change.

For instance, if we go back to the very beginning of the human problem in Genesis 3, we can see how the "law" meted out only condemnation. Adam's disobedience resulted in a curse. He brought death into the world. But the Lord holds out hope nonetheless. Many see the "first gospel" in Genesis 3:15, where the serpent's doom is foretold by the same heel he will bite—perhaps a foreshadowing of the cross of Christ, which appears on the surface as a failure but is, in fact, a victory. But we also see in Genesis 3:21 how the Lord covers the shame and nakedness of the first couple with animal skins. Fig leaves wouldn't cut it. They could not cover themselves with the work of their own hands; the Lord himself would cover them, and something had to die.

From there onward, the recurring theme of grace is woven throughout the old covenant Scriptures. Think of the freeing of the Israelites from Egyptian bondage, climactically achieved through the final plague of the bloody Passover. The law was not delivered to God's people until after their liberation. They were not set free *by* their obedience but rather *to* their obedience. In other words, they were graciously led out of slavery by God to receive his commandments and pursue free worship of him.

God's covenantal faithfulness to his sinful people is a recurring reminder, even as a shadow of the Messiah to come, that salvation cannot be found in our own strength. Abraham was not justified by his works, in other words, but by his faith in the one to come. Abraham was, ultimately, saved by Jesus.

The entire story line of the Scriptures, in fact, culminates in the proclamation of Christ. He is the point of the entire Book. As Paul says in 2 Corinthians 1:20, "For all the promises of God find their Yes in him" (ESV).

Even Jesus preaches himself from the Old Testament. In John 5:39, he rebukes the false teachers, saying, "You search the Scriptures because you think that in them you have eternal life; and it is they that bear witness about me" (ESV). After his resurrection, Jesus sidles up next to a couple of his disciples on the road to Emmaus and basically preaches a self-centered exposition of the entire Old Testament to them (Luke 24:27).

After Christ's ascension, the very first sermon of the newly birthed Christian Church was Peter's on the day of Pentecost, which basically amounts to a Christ-centered exposition of Joel 2 and Psalm 16. In Galatians 3:24–25, Paul says that the Old Testament was our "tutor," in essence an instructor training us to long for Christ. The entire book of Hebrews, in fact, amounts to an exposition of the old covenant and its fulfillment in Jesus.

*The point of the whole Bible is Jesus.* So it is possible to preach the Bible in an unchristian way, even if we ourselves are Christians preaching to Christians in a Christian church. If we do not preach Christ from the text, we are not preaching a Christian sermon. We can tack on a gospel presentation to the end of a sermon (and certainly a tacked-on gospel is better than no gospel), but if we have not preached Christ from the text, the sermon itself is not a Christian sermon.

I will say more on this in our preaching chapters, but for now let us resolve to maintain a distinctly Christian way of understanding the whole Bible. Let's study it for ourselves and for our flocks with Christ as our heart's central longing and our mind's central vision. Let's preach it with Christ as the center, for he is the apex and the sum of all its riches.

## Gospel-Centrality Produces Transformation

Personal transformation often becomes a chief concern for ministry. From our fears about ineffectual sermons to the mundane rehearsing of the same advice in countless counseling and discipleship meetings, we strive toward the goal of people changing. We are invested in transformation. It's the whole point of Christianity to love Christ and become more like him. I hope you are beginning to see that the means to this end are counterintuitive. Indeed, the *end* is Christ himself and the *means* is Christ himself!

Consider these words from Paul from his pastoral letter to his young protégé Titus: "For the grace of God has appeared, bringing salvation for all people, training us to renounce ungodliness and worldly passions, and to live self-controlled, upright, and godly lives in the present age" (2:11–12 ESV). If we were to ask the average Christian, "What is it that trains people to renounce ungodliness?"—in other words, "How do you get people to behave in a way that glorifies God?"—most would reply with some variation of the law, with imperatives. "You tell them what to do." But this isn't what Paul says at all. It's totally counterintuitive; in fact, it's totally supernatural! Paul says it is *grace* that trains us. Somehow, the message of "It is finished!" empowers us to get to work.

Elsewhere Paul writes, "Therefore, my beloved, as you have always obeyed, so now, not only as in my presence but much more in my absence, work out your own salvation with fear and trembling, for it is God who works in you, both to will and to work for his good pleasure" (Phil 2:12–13 ESV). Verse 12 sounds ominous enough. When was the last time you experienced fear and trembling in your pursuit of obedience? But good news! Paul says we are only working *out* what God has already worked *in*. And what has he worked in? The "word of life," to which he admonishes us to "hold fast" (2:16 ESV). And the holding fast has tremendous effects. Indeed, the more we center on the gospel, the more fruit we begin to see in our lives. The more we abide in Jesus, the more like him we become.

Back in 2 Corinthians 3, where Paul explicates the law/gospel dynamic, ends on this climactic note: "And we all, with unveiled face, beholding the glory of the Lord, are being transformed into the same image from one degree of glory to another. For this comes from the Lord who is the Spirit" (3:18 ESV). Notice that while efforts toward obedience are good and honorable (when directed to God's glory not our own), this is not the named power for transformation in Christlikeness. No, it is "beholding the glory of the Lord" that transforms us into his image. Seeing Jesus makes us more like Jesus. Seeing his glory changes us.

We are good pastors if we are concerned that people become more like our Savior. This means that we take discipleship seriously. But we have missed the boat if we aim to work toward this without consistently and primarily pointing people to Jesus, holding up his glory so that people can be changed by it.

I can remember the Sunday this realization crashed into me mid-sermon. I had prided myself on my gospel-centrality. But I had, ironically, become law-centered about gospel-centrality! In other words, I was in the midst of chastising my congregation, telling them to "Be gospel-centered" and "Be awed by grace!" These are good admonitions. But another Luther quote flashed into my mind, I think from the Spirit's prompting: "It's the supreme art of the devil that he can make the law out of gospel."[2] I was being legalistic about gospel-centrality.

I cannot simply berate people into centering on grace; I need to hold it up for them to see. I can't simply tell people to be awed by Christ; I need to hold up Christ's glory so that they can be. If we want people to be more changed toward the image of Christ, we will center on the only power for this change—the gospel of Christ.

## Gospel-Centrality Shapes Pastoral Identity

The glory of Christ is our only power for ministry. Therefore, the glory of Christ is our true strength as ministers.

Do we know that we can quit apologizing for Jesus? Do we know that Jesus does not need our help? In fact, we need *his* . . .

. . . on Sunday nights when we are bone tired and yet can't sleep.

. . . on Monday mornings when we're weary and just feel bruised, having been broken open before our people the day before.

. . . when the emails sit there in the inbox, and the voicemails pile up.

. . . when you're looking at the ministry week ahead of you, and the boulder you rolled up the hill the week before has rolled back down to the bottom.

In all of these moments, what do we need? We've already seen briefly that this is what we all need: a beholding of the glory of Christ, *who comes with might* (Isa 40:10 ESV). Second Peter 1:3–4 tells us, "His divine power has granted to us all things that pertain to life and godliness, through the knowledge of him who called us to his own glory and excellence, by which he has granted to us his

---

2. Martin Luther, *Martin Luther's Table Talks*, ed. Henry F. French (Minneapolis: Fortress, 2017), 15.

precious and very great promises, so that through them you may become partakers of the divine nature" (ESV).

Pastors, when the breath of dying people is in our nostrils, the flimsy spirituality of popular religion will be of no use. It will fail to comfort or provide hope. The couples whose marriages are failing, the addicts, the victims of abuse, the doubting and hurting and broken, and the dying need to know that "the Lord God comes with might"—that he is mighty to save!

It is amazing how many pastors waste their ministry, and even their lives, seeking to be impressive, to be seen, to be celebrated, to be themselves followed. Others may never see tremendous growth, exterior success, or the status that comes with platform, but if they are bringing glory to Christ—if we are getting up on the mountain to say over and over again, "Behold Your God!"—not a thing about them is wasted, because the mission of the Spirit of God is to maximize the glory of Christ over all the universe. It is not our giftedness or our achievements that make us strong but submitting our weakness to the mighty Christ!

So, we don't need to get our own way. We don't need to be a big deal. We don't need to be the smartest or most spiritual one in the room. When we take to the pulpit, we don't need to "bring the fire" or "bring the thunder" or *whatever*; we simply need to bring Christ! We must not be like the rooster who thinks the sun is coming up because he's crowing. The sun of righteousness, the radiance of God's glory, is not commanded or conjured. He is worshiped; he is obeyed; he is proclaimed. *Pastor, Christ is your true strength.* Yes, the strength for the gospel-centered pastor is in the very pastoring of Christ.

> He will tend his flock like a shepherd;
>> he will gather the lambs in his arms;
> he will carry them in his bosom,
>> and gently lead those that are with young. (Isa 40:11 ESV)

What a comfort this is to those who are uncomfortable with them-selves and discontent with their own power. Never forget, shepherd, that you are—first and foremost—a sheep yourself. There is not a single one of us who is too big, too strong, too gifted, or too well-regarded to be one of Christ's little lambs.

The older I get, the more I long to sit on the lap of Jesus Christ and have him hold me. I don't care what that makes you think of my masculinity or maturity—I want to be held by my shepherd. I want him to carry me in his bosom and gently lead me. This is the picture of the true shepherd that we enter into as pastors. There are times when a shepherd needs to get out in front; there are times when the rod of correction must come in, when the sheep need to be driven; but the big portrait—the tone and texture of biblical shep-herding—is comforting, carrying, and gently leading the sheep.

On what will you place your trust this very moment for the vindi-cation of your ministry? What are you worshiping *right now*? When we are angling for platform, for recognition, for pats on the back, for reverence, for validation and fulfillment and justification in any-thing but Christ, it's like a squirming in his arms, trying to break free. The only result is that we will fall.

John Calvin says of Isaiah 40:11, "We must therefore lay aside our fierceness, and permit ourselves to be tamed."[3] This is, in fact, the overarching qualification embedded in those biblical qualifi-cations listed in 1 Timothy 3, Titus 1, and 1 Peter 5, covered in the previous chapter. What those characteristics compose is a man who has been won by, submitted to, and formed in Christ's very self.

Are you bucking against the gentle arms of the shepherd? Are you kicking at his tender leading?

The Lord your God loves you with an unfailing love. He will be your comfort. He will be your strength. He will be your power. Now you don't have to worry about what they think of you so much. Now

---

3. John Calvin, *Calvin's Commentaries*, vol. 8, *Isaiah 33–66* (Grand Rapids: Baker, 2009), 216.

you don't have to define yourself by your stats. Now you don't have to measure your validation by your best sermon or your high attendance or your giving campaign or your PR among the congregation. He will be your vindication too! He will be your validation. Your identity is secure in him purely by grace.

How centering the gospel is! When outside is all conflict or chaos, and inside is all confusion and concern, Christ is upholding the pastor with his powerful word. To steward well the mystery of God's grace in Christ in ministry to others, then, we must steward it well unto ourselves, to our own hearts and minds. As Luther says, you must know this article well. You must have it as the central coursing heart of your ministry. Resolve to know nothing except Jesus Christ and him crucified.

## For Reflection

1. How would you summarize the gospel in one sentence? Explain why you include each part.
2. How would you summarize the gospel message in a paragraph (in three sentences)?
3. How would you define gospel-centrality, and what are its major implications for pastoral ministry?
4. Why do you think the concept of gospel-centrality sounds like a "foreign language" to some preachers or churches?
5. Is it possible to be legalistic about gospel-centrality? If so, what would this look like?

## For Further Study:

Bridges, Jerry. *Transforming Grace: Living Confidently in God's Unfailing Love.* 3rd ed. Colorado Springs: NavPress, 2017.
    Few authors in the modern era have been as fixated on the

gospel as power for sanctification as Bridges was. This work is a representative sample from his blessed fixation.

Owen, John. *The Glory of Christ.* Carlisle, PA: Banner of Truth, 1994.

This Puritan masterpiece deliciously rehearses on every page the heart change that comes from beholding the power of the gospel.

Sproul, R. C. *Getting the Gospel Right: The Tie That Binds Evangelicals Together.* Grand Rapids: Baker, 1999.

Largely a review of the Protestant view of justification by faith over and against the unbiblical soteriology of Roman Catholicism, this book is a helpful reminder of the crucial doctrine undergirding the true biblical gospel.

# CHAPTER 3

# WORSHIPING

Every age and segment of the church faces its own moments of crisis. For Christians in the West, a major threat we could point to in the present moment is biblical illiteracy in the church—it's occurring at a rate that is unprecedented since the invention of the printing press. We are more resourced than we've ever been, and yet we've never been more ignorant. Perhaps we could also point to the rise of the prosperity gospel, that heretical blend of legalism and magic that has infiltrated many corners of evangelicalism and is now being exported to the third world. Or in the United States, specifically, one could highlight the unholy wedding of Christianity and political ambition, a potent syncretism that fuels idolatry among both right-wingers and leftists.

But the problems in our churches are not primarily political or cultural. They are spiritual and formational. These are discipleship problems, and discipleship problems are worship problems. The fundamental problem is one of disordered worship. We are ambivalent about God's Word because we don't hallow him. We succumb to the prosperity gospel because we don't know him. We surrender to political idolatry because we don't trust him. Our desire for truth, provision, and power is directed elsewhere. Disordered worship is the major disease threatening every local church. It may not manifest itself in any of the ailments listed above, but the churches we pastor will, regardless, be infected with it. And so will we.

In fact, as one who sets an example for the flock (1 Peter 5:3), you may be setting the course for others' disordered worship with your own. The pastor who majors in moralistic preaching is forming moralistic impulses in his congregation. The pastor who prides himself on creative production is shaping a consumeristic flock that is inordinately enamored with entertainment. The pastor who uses the Word sparsely or superficially is implicitly instructing his people to see the Bible as optional—like a spice to be added to life but not bread on which to subsist.

As pastor, we are lead worshipers. We may not know how to read music or carry a tune in a bucket, but this is not ultimately about singing. It is about the passion of our hearts and the concerted interest of our ministry. What and how we're worshiping will catch on. Note well, pastor, that our people won't necessarily get excited about what we tell them to be excited about. They will instead, over time, become excited about what we ourselves are excited about. You can tell people to center on the gospel, for instance, but if it's clear that your passion is the law, you will cultivate a law-heavy people. Whatever the pastors are, the church will eventually become.

Oh, there are plenty of ministers aflame with *something*. We do not lack cheerleaders, pep-talkers, motivational speakers, visionary dreamers, and the like. But all the enthusiasm and creativity are wasted if they are not directed Godward. We must take care to warm our hearts by God's Word, ensuring that we become fueled by the gospel of grace into a passion exemplary to those we lead. This does not really have anything to do with our talent or education. Some of the most talented and educated ministers in the world have been dry as old rice when it comes to matters of grace. You don't need a diploma or an audience to cultivate vibrant worship, just a heart and God's grace.

A young Englishman training for the ministry is said to have complained to his instructing pastor, "I'm not the sort of man who could set the Thames on fire," to which his elder replied, "Young man, I'm not concerned about your setting the Thames on fire. What I want to know is this: if I grabbed you by the scruff of your neck and dropped you into that river, would it sizzle?" In other words, the fire of your holiness—your passion for God—is far more important than the fire of your oratory or leadership skills.

Paul reminds his pastoral pupil, Timothy, "to fan into flame the gift of God" (2 Tim 1:6). Great care and diligence must be taken to cultivate a heart of worship, for your own sake and for the sake of your flock. You need this, and they need this from you.

So how do you get there? How do you fan that flame? What does a worshiping pastor look like? Let us draw out three vital aspects of pastoral worship from one of the most worshipful books of the New Testament: the epistle of the Lord's brother Jude.

## Adorational Study

How early in your day do you warm yourself by the Word of God?

Like many other fools, I use my phone for my alarm clock. Picking up my phone before I've even sat upright or set my feet on the floor used to mean not just turning my alarm off but quickly and casually checking email, looking at my calendar appointments and obligations for the day, and even scrolling through social media apps. For the longest time, this meant that even if my first task of the morning was time spent reading the Bible, I typically came to God's Word with other words already occupying my mind.

The Holy Spirit was kind to convict me about whose words take first priority in my day. I still use my phone as my clock, but the very first thing I do after turning off the alarm in the morning, before I've even sat up, is open up one of my Bible apps and ponder whatever the Lord has for me that morning. My substantive Bible study time will come later when I'm more fully awake, but I still want his words to be the first words I hear each day. This practice is not primarily a function of study, though it's usually impossible not to think for a while on the passages I'm encountering in these moments. It is primarily a function of worship. I want my daily thoughts and affections to have their agenda set by God. And I want to bring this spirit of worship with me later when I dive into Bible study more deeply.

Writing to a largely Jewish church that had been infiltrated by a sort of heresy that had led them into licentiousness, Jude points his prophetic finger at the sort of shepherds who are cancerous with disordered worship.

> These are hidden reefs at your love feasts, as they feast with you without fear, shepherds feeding themselves; waterless clouds, swept along by winds; fruitless trees in late autumn, twice dead, uprooted; wild waves of the sea, casting up the foam of their own shame; wandering stars, for whom the gloom of utter darkness has been reserved forever. (Jude 12–13 ESV)

This is what you and I *don't* want to be: empty, dry, hollow, thin, blown about by wind and thrown about by tides. And this frailty is not simply a symptom of thin theology. It is the result of flimsy worship. In fact, for Jude, these two are inextricably connected—and they should be for us as well. Jude wants Christians to be neither unstirred in affections for Christ nor uninterested in the course correction of sound doctrine. He wants right doctrine that stirs affections.

And if this central revelation about bad shepherds is a huge part of the problem, then it stands to reason that good shepherds are part of the solution. Good shepherds are those who stuff themselves full of the glory of God in the Word. They are "true worshipers," as Jesus said, those who "worship the Father in spirit and truth" (John 4:23 ESV).

Pastor, *your pursuit of theology is not simply for information but for adoration.* But of course, getting to the point of doctrinally fueled adoration assumes you are engaged in the work of theology in the first place. "Beloved, although I was very eager to write to you about our common salvation, I found it necessary to write appealing to you to contend for the faith that was once for all delivered to the saints" (Jude 3 ESV). The apostle is writing against the disordered worship of sensuality by urging believers to contend for the faith. In 1 Timothy 1:8–11, we learn that sensual sins, passions of the flesh, are contrary to "sound doctrine" and "the gospel of the glory of the blessed God" (ESV). What we learn in these passages and others is that bad doctrine doesn't just affect what we know, but *what we do.* Your theology fuels your worship. Every behavior problem is a belief problem. A wonky theology leads inevitably to wonky behavior. Thus, good theology is an antidote to bad worship.

And yet, Jude is not saying that a correct doctrinal statement is all we need for the Christian life. In fact, quite the opposite. You don't avoid licentiousness by indulging in dry spirituality. Our whole selves are involved: "You shall love the LORD your God with all your heart and with all your soul and with all your might" (Deut 6:5 ESV). Jesus calls this the greatest commandment (Matt 22:37–38).

Loving God with all of our minds certainly means more than theological study, of course, but it certainly does not mean less than that. We all have known pastors who are known for their intellectual acumen who did not bring love to bear, whether in their relation to God or their relation to others. Occasionally, all of us end up being one of those pastors. But Paul says that all the knowledge in the world is worthless without love (1 Cor 13:2). Do you remember to bring your heart to your studies? Do you steward your theological gains toward great affections for Christ?

Devoted pastors are not those who have come to place their trust in vague spiritual platitudes; they are those who have come to place their trust by the real Spirit in the real Savior, Jesus, as proclaimed in the specific words of the powerful gospel. A pastor shows himself authentic by growing as a teacher and "rightly handling the word of truth" (2 Tim 2:15 ESV). Rightly stewarding the Word means staring into the mystery of Christ with our minds and submitting to it with our hearts so our souls can be changed and charged.

This is why we must pursue theological robustness, not just in our pulpit preaching, but also in our church's music and in our church's prayers, both corporate and private. "Authentic worship" has become one of the buzzwords du jour in the evangelical scene. However, authentic worship has much less to do with whether our musicians' style or "vibe" communicates cultural relevance and much more to do with whether their songs and spirit conform to the ancient tradition of divine reality.

But theological study goes deeper than simply authenticating our worship as true and godly—it also fuels our worship. The study is adorational. We are turning the corner from theology to doxology, as Jude does at the end of his letter. We are changed deeply in heart, and therefore behavior, when we seek deeply after the things of God with our brains. The Bible says so: "Do not be conformed to this world," Paul writes, "but be transformed by the renewal of your mind, that by testing you may discern what is the will of God, what is good and acceptable and perfect" (Rom 12:2 ESV). The transformation begins with a renewing of our minds. As I heard John Piper once say, "The theological mind exists to throw logs into the furnace of our affections for Christ." Along these same lines, Jonathan Edwards identified theological study as a sign of revival in *The Distinguishing Marks of a Work of the Spirit of God*.

We want the blessing of the psalmist, then, who doesn't simply read the word, but "delights" in it and consequently "meditates" on it all day long (Ps 1:2). He is meditating precisely *because* he delights in it! He finds, as he exults in Christ in his study, as he adores the living God in his exegetical sharpening, that like those disciples on the Emmaus road, his heart burns within him (Luke 24:32).

Adorational study of God's Word deepens not just our knowledge of God, but also our love for him. The more we read, study, meditate on, and prayerfully apply the Word of God, the more we will find ourselves in awe of him. We often fear the opposite danger—that the more we "study God," the more we think we will scrutinize him into smallness, placing him in a doctrinal box of our own intellectual design. Certainly, some do this. But those with a heart captured by God's gospel will discover the opposite is actually true as they also apply their mind to his ways and wonders. Like a great ship on the horizon, the closer we sail toward him, the larger he looms. When our face is pressed against his bosom, we don't find that our closeness to him reduces him to smallness at all; rather, the breadth of his majesty and wonder stretches far out of our eyesight, running as far as east is from west.

## Prayerful Preparation

A friend of mine once noted that, as he traveled far and wide to visit churches in his work as a children's ministry consultant, he encountered few worship gatherings that featured much prayer. Perfunctory prayers may be offered as transitions between songs or at the initiation of the offertory, but dedicated time to offer concentrated prayer seemed to be going the way of the dodo. I suppose that prayerless church services are likely the product of prayerless church leaders.

Another friend of mine says pastors ought to know what the carpet in their study smells like. What he means is that the pastor should be so accustomed to being prostrate before the Lord that he can practically taste the dirt and the burnt rubber from the vacuum belt in his mouth just thinking about prayer. You use your desk often enough, pastor. Do you use your carpet?

As we have already established, the power you need to pastor is not derived from within. It is a gift from the alien righteousness of

Christ. It comes from God's Spirit. Thus, our attention to God's Word must be drenched in prayerful surrender.

Prayer is essentially acknowledged helplessness, the act by which we recognize that everything we need must be graciously given by God. Therefore, every day, all throughout the ministry week, the worshipful pastor is spilling his guts to God in acknowledgment that anything he has to give his flock cannot come from himself but from on high. Even when our weak prayers feel like drudgery, they should be seen as going up the mountain to get glory. We cannot conjure it up ourselves. It must be granted and reflected.

"But you, beloved," Jude writes, "building yourselves up in your most holy faith and praying in the Holy Spirit, keep yourselves in the love of God" (Jude 20 ESV). The parallel here between "faith" and "prayer in the Spirit" is notable. Faith is an empty hand and prayer is a confession of need.

In our devotional times and in our sermon preparation, as the Scriptures take us out of our depth, we pray for understanding, for insight, and for help in taking them to heart. Pray that God would empower you to follow his Word and give you pastoral insight to the needs of your people. Intercede for them even as you cook up the expository meal for them to eat. Make the sermon prep an act of love, both toward God and toward your congregation.

The work of sermon preparation should also be an act of love for the lost! Pray that God would awaken souls through your ministry, that he would bring the dead to life. Pray that your words be used to amplify God's Word, which ushers people trapped in the darkness into his marvelous light.

Prepare yourself for ministry prayerfully. Embrace this posture of humility and beg for God's help. Plead with him for strength, for unction, for revival. Petition him for healing and deliverance. Pray as though, if God weren't to help you, you couldn't get anything done that mattered. Don't be like Uzziah, who was marvelously helped "until he became powerful" (2 Chr 26:15). Trust that God's strength is perfected in weakness and own the expressed weakness of prayer. This is another important way we fan that flame. If the Word of God brings the fire, prayer is perhaps the stacking of the wood. We are opening ourselves to God's power, exposing ourselves to God's holiness, and bringing ourselves before his mercy.

Luke tells us that Jesus often withdrew to lonely places to pray (5:16). If the Good Shepherd needed that, why wouldn't we? The worshiping pastor is a praying pastor. He is a prayer-*full* pastor.

## Exultational Exposition

Do you want to counteract the erosion of biblical literacy in your church? The subtle infiltration of the prosperity gospel? The siren songs of all our culture's idols?

Your congregation will note what you are excited about. And if you do not preach, teach, disciple, and counsel worshipfully, they will pick up on the boredom you don't even mean to convey.

It is remarkable that Jude's antiheresy tract basically ends with a worship song!

> Now to him who is able to keep you from stumbling and to present you blameless before the presence of his glory with great joy, to the only God, our Savior, through Jesus Christ our Lord, be glory, majesty, dominion, and authority, before all time and now and forever. Amen. (Jude 24–25 ESV)

The apostle has turned the corner from theology to doxology. And this tells us something very important about our preaching and teaching.

It is not enough in our preaching to simply provide a running commentary on the text. Sometimes, this is not even an effective means of biblical exposition, as we may miss the larger context. More concerning, it may not be an effectual means of transformation, as many verse-by-verse sermons neglect to expose the glory of Christ in the text, keeping back from hearers their only hope for heart change. Do not be that shepherd about whom Jude warns who takes to the pulpit feeding on himself, a waterless cloud, a mist with no rain, a blower of hot air, a dry branch with no root.

Instead, your exposition must be fraught with exultation. The aim of the sermon is no different from the aim of the rest of the service: leading sinners to worship God. Merely filling congregants' brains with Bible facts and entertaining their flesh with inspirational stories will only exacerbate the problem of disordered worship.

Treat your sermon like a call to worship. Treat your sermon like it is itself an act of worship.

Every seasoned preacher knows the experience of unction. Every now and again, in the Spirit's kindness, he allows us, even in the midst of going through our preplanned outline or manuscript, to find a sort of jet stream where he more or less takes over. We are speaking, but we sense his presence and feel his power. He is giving us the words to say, and every word is like an arrow to the hearts of our people—arrows that bring life and warmth! They are like the illuminating beams of the one who is the radiance of the glory of God.

Never has this unction been dispensed to me when I am dryly reciting facts or covering some other perfunctory matter. Never has it come when I, myself, remain unmoved by what I am declaring. It comes as I worship, as if I am chipping gleefully away at the dam of the congregation's affections and my own, and suddenly the Lord simply blows the stones away himself. We feel that living water rush.

So, pastor: study yourself hot. Pray yourself full. Preach Christ passionately and gratuitously.

But remember that preaching is not only or primarily about feelings. It is about the proclamation of the truth. It is not a-theological. Good preaching is replete with glorious doctrine. But it is not business as usual; it is the fruit of exposition that is exultational. And it is to that exposition we will more fully turn in the next two chapters.

# For Reflection

1. Do you struggle more with devotional study of the Bible or with intimate prayer with God? Why?
2. Why are both Bible study and solitary prayer crucial for the flourishing of a pastor and his congregation?
3. What is your plan to develop in the areas of personal devotion where you feel weak?
4. What does a worshipful study of the Scriptures look like?
5. How does the gospel inform your understanding of prayer? How does the gospel *drive* prayer?

# For Further Study:

Augustine. *The Confessions of Saint Augustine.* Translated by John K. Ryan. New York: Image, 1960.

Not on pastoral ministry per se, this autobiography-slash-devotional-theology is the greatest example of a worshipful heart brought to the study of doctrine. Read *The Confessions* to discover what exulting in the gospel looks like.

Bunyan, John. *Prayer.* Carlisle, PA: Banner of Truth, 1965.

The author of the classic *Pilgrim's Progress* here masterfully aids believers in approaching the throne of grace and "praying in the Spirit."

Peterson, Eugene. *The Contemplative Pastor: Returning to the Art of Spiritual Direction.* Grand Rapids: Eerdmans, 1993.

Few voices in the contemporary field seem as skilled at pastoring pastors as the late Peterson. This work showcases the height of his powers.

# CHAPTER 4

# PREACHING *Part 1*

There are many ways to rile up church people. One way I discovered quite by accident was suggesting they didn't need to take notes while I preached. You would have thought I'd said they all had two heads. What I thought I was doing was relieving them of a burden. What they thought I was doing was stifling their ability to learn. And what I learned through the process is that a great many church folk don't know what a sermon is.

A great number of preachers don't seem to know, either. I faced similar disgruntlement more recently when I suggested, based on scientific research, that the use of PowerPoint slides during the sermon does not actually help people retain information. More than twenty years ago, it would not have occurred to anyone that what preaching really needed was overhead screens highlighting key points or sermon excerpts. People seemed to manage just fine. Today, it is taken as a given that effective preaching necessitates not only more bite-size sermons but also an entire audio-visual "experience."

The use of overhead visuals in preaching is not a hill I care to die on. But it's worth noting that the arguments used to rebut even scientific data on the ineffectiveness of such means tend to reflect a conception of preaching and of the sermon that is unique to our modern age.

This chapter will reach beyond these contemporary innovations to discover, *What is a sermon? What is preaching?* In the next chapter, I will turn more to the practicalities of sermon preparation and delivery, but in this chapter I wish to focus on a more foundational matter: the nature of Christian preaching.

## What Is Preaching?

Some of the note takers and PowerPoint users seem to think of the Sunday sermon as a kind of informational download, a spiritual lecture. And indeed, no preaching is complete without teaching. The one skill set mentioned in the biblical list of qualifications for eldership is the ability to teach, and this ability must be brought to bear in the pastoral "ministry of the Word." But there is nevertheless a biblical distinction drawn between teaching and preaching.

There are several instances in the New Testament where preaching and teaching are distinguished from each other: Matthew 11:1, Luke 20:1, Acts 5:42, Acts 15:35, and 1 Timothy 5:17. In 2 Timothy 1:11, Paul says he was appointed a preacher and a teacher. Certainly, all preaching includes teaching—as in 2 Timothy 4:2 where Paul lists teaching, reproving, rebuking, and exhorting all as aspects of "preaching the word"—but Christian preaching, especially preaching in the Lord's Day worship gathering, isn't synonymous with teaching a lesson. Getting information across is important and necessary, but it's not the main point.

Biblically speaking, the concept of preaching is connected to the idea of *heralding*. But heralding what? Primarily the good news of Jesus Christ! The category of preaching seems especially reserved for the work of evangelism—announcing that the grace of God in Christ is available to all who will repent of their sin and believe in him.

Because of this, some would argue that what takes place in a church setting should not be considered preaching at all, but rather teaching, reserving preaching for what takes place "in the outside world" as we minister to the lost. The major problem with this is the assumption that the church does not need the gospel proclaimed to them. As I've hopefully established in the previous chapters, no Christian "moves on" from the gospel. It is not just the grounds and power for our conversion experience, but also for our daily rootedness in Christ's righteousness and the ongoing work of becoming more like Jesus through discipleship to him. The Christian church needs constant reevangelization, and thus the Christian church needs preaching.

My working definition of preaching for the last decade or so has been "proclamation that exults in the exposing of God's glory in Christ." Each component of this definition is important, I think, to the preparation and delivery of the sermon.

The nature of the sermon is primarily proclamation. The preacher must teach, explaining the text and providing background, insights, and context, but the teaching serves the preaching. In other words, the sermon is not a lecture. It is not a lesson. Still less is it performance art or a half-time speech. Preaching is not inspirational storytelling. Preaching is a declaration of the oracles of God. It is a proclamation of the mystery now revealed through Jesus Christ. The pastor must bring his soul to bear on the souls of his people through the ministry of the Word.

This is where the exultation comes in. Preaching is proclamation that exults in Christ, through the Word, over his grace. The sermon is an act of worship and has worship as its aim—that hearers would come to enjoy Christ more or for the first time.

The normative means of this enjoyment is encountering the Word of God. It is God's Word that is "living and active" (Heb 4:12 ESV). This is where the "exposing" part of my definition of preaching comes in. It is reflective of the work of expositional preaching, which means preaching that "exposits" (or *exposes*) a text of

Scripture for its audience. The preacher works in and through a biblical text—whether it's a verse or two or a larger passage—to "give the sense" (Neh 8:8 ESV) so that people can understand the Scriptures and have the opportunity to be convicted, comforted, and changed by them.

Ultimately, this is all martialed toward the only power to change, what every person must behold in order to have the opportunity to know God and his love and to love him in return: the glory of God in Christ. As Paul says in 2 Corinthians 3:18, it is only by beholding the glory of Christ that we can be transformed into his image. Christian preaching, then, doesn't simply provide a running commentary on a Bible passage; preaching provides, through the text, a hearing of the gospel in the hopes of a seeing of the glory of God in Christ.

Preaching in the Sunday service is the pastor's way of reorienting his flock back around the giver and sustainer of life. It is the paramount event of the church's week, the regular pivot point for the body's love of God and ministry to itself and others. It is important each week to have the preacher say in some way, shape, or form, "Behold your God!" and "Thus saith the Lord!" We need a word from on high. We are lost without a report from heaven. This is what the preacher brings to us.

We must consistently reorient ourselves around the purpose of the preaching task as we go about the weekly work of sermon preparation and delivery. But when we begin composing sermons regularly, it can be difficult to gauge if we are staying on track. With this challenge before us, we now turn to consider the components we should look for in the finished product as a way of determining not just if our sermon is "good," but if it is fundamentally Christian.

## The Elements of Christian Preaching

The Scriptures are the most precious treasure entrusted to the church, and in them we find the message of the gospel. It alone holds the power of salvation, the power for the maturation of the church, and the power for the conquest of the earth by Christ's kingdom. Ministries wither and pastors fade, but the Word of God will stand forever.

Unapologetically, then, we should affirm that the primary task of the pastor is to preach and teach the Bible. Preaching is in fact a vital work of pastoral care.

But what are the basic elements of biblical preaching? How do you know you're preaching a Christian sermon and not simply giving a religious or spiritual lecture?

In service of the idea of preaching as proclamation that exults in the exposing of God's glory in Christ, there are some basic elements that should be present in every sermon. Gifted preachers can certainly add to these criteria, but they are nevertheless helpful for providing a fundamental sense of Christian preaching. I have phrased them as questions that you may ask of your sermons.

## Is Your Sermon Contextual?

Notice that this is a more specific question than simply asking if the message is *textual*. Many preachers employ Bible verses in their sermons, and by this they determine that their sermon is based on a biblical text. But putting some Bible verses in your sermon is not the same thing as preaching the Bible. Moreover, while it is entirely appropriate to simply explicate one or two verses in your sermon, there remains the danger in such small selections of not capturing the import of even those one or two verses *if they're taken out of context.* Think of the fellow who preaches a whole Mother's Day sermon from John 19:27. He has loaded up all the weight of a Hallmark moment onto a verse that, in context, speaks to the love Jesus shared even in his death.

You will miss important interpretative information by focusing on isolated slivers of the Bible. Every biblical text should be interpreted according to its immediate context, and every immediate context should be interpreted according to the greater context of the gospel story line of Scripture. As the old preacher's dictum goes: "A text without a context is a pretext for a prooftext."

One way to avoid this is for preachers to make sure the biblical text drives what they are saying and not the other way around. And you know you're being driven by the text when you are considering how it is informed by its context.

## Is Your Sermon Convictional?

Convictional rhetoric is key to the nature of preaching as proclamation. Ask about your message points in particular but also about the exposition generally: "Am I expressing declarations of truth?" The import of a Christian sermon is not simply to raise questions and coddle felt needs but to give answers and announcements. Authentic Christian preaching comes with conviction about who God is, what God has done, and what this means for you and me.

Convictional preaching is weighted with authority. It does not hem and haw about sin and the law. Convictional preaching is sober about the realities of hell and God's wrath. Convictional preaching doesn't cater to the world's values or a congregation's consumeristic impulses. Convictional preaching doesn't avoid or soften the essential and orthodox doctrines of historic Christianity. And perhaps most essentially, convictional preaching means we preach the written Word of God as inspired and infallible, sufficient and supernatural, living and life-giving.

Do you have a word for us, preacher? Are you just throwing stuff out there to see what sticks, or do you have a word? Whether he says it or not, every preacher should begin his sermon as if he has a message from the very throne room of God to deliver. It is urgent. It is important. It is authoritative. It is a matter of life and death. This doesn't mean the preacher must always be somber. Remember to exult! (See question 4 below, as well.) But it does mean the preacher feels the gravity of the glory of God and the souls at stake in the hearing about it. Don't entertain us; bring us a word.

## Is Your Sermon Clear?

When we bring a message from God, we must do it in the language of our people. A sermon that people find difficult to understand is not a good sermon! The preacher may be impressing people with theological jargon, complex doctrinal concepts, and long trains of philosophical thought but, if it isn't understandable, it will all amount to a distraction from the Lord. *Make it plain, preacher. Simple, but not simple-minded. Deep, but not over our heads.*

There are two important aspects of clarity: clear speaking and clear understanding. Good preaching isn't dumbed down, of course, and often stretches hearers' intellects. But it is best to stretch hearers' intellects with big thoughts of God, not big words of preachers. The specific contexts of our communities and congregations can certainly factor into what kind of illustrations we use, what kind of vocabulary we employ, and so on. But just remember that even if we're preaching at Harvard, making it difficult to understand the Bible—much less respond to it—does not validate our homiletical prowess!

Sometimes, I think this is why some preachers stick to the King James Version: the archaic language is difficult for modern ears to make sense of, and because of this, the preacher can pretend to be some specially anointed exegetical priest and repository of divine knowledge. For your own preaching, I suggest using a reliable and relatively modern Bible translation that will prove intelligible and profitable for your people's use in their own study apart from your teaching on Sundays.

An important part of clarity is defining our terms. I remember when a long-time church member and future elder made some reference to "being a good Berean" in the adult Bible study I was teaching one morning. There were lots of nodding heads in the study circle, as most attendees understood the reference to the Bereans who measured the things Paul and Silas preached against the Scriptures to test the trustworthiness of their teaching (Acts 17:10–11). But there was one woman in the room who was a new believer. She was not nodding. She had no idea what the reference was about. But she didn't raise her hand to ask. So I gently said to my friend, "Could you explain what a Berean is?" and he gladly did.

Remember, preacher, that there are people in the room who don't know the lingo. Know your audience. And then help your audience know God's Word. Make it clear.

## Is Your Sermon Compassionate?

What is our motivation in preaching? Is it to comfort God's people and speak tenderly to them? Is it to tell them their iniquity is pardoned, and their warfare is over? Many preachers engage in a kind of passionate preaching. Rarer is *com*passionate preaching. This is the kind of passion that erupts from love for souls. For souls, generally, but also for the specific souls in our congregations. This question for our sermon evaluation is simply asking, *Are you preaching out of love?*

This doesn't mean that every sermon must have the same emotional tone. Different texts carry the tones of their contexts. Some biblical texts call for rebuke and some call for rejoicing. Some call for both. One of the great advantages of expository preaching is that it helps us preach according to the grain of the text. But it's possible to bring emotion to a sermon that is either completely unwarranted by the text itself or totally unhelpful to the aim of helping people see Jesus. Some preachers seem to think that preaching means yelling. (Know that if all of your sentences end with exclamation points then, effectively, none of them does.)

To preach with compassion is not simply to preach happy or sad or with deep emotions. That's all well and good. Preaching, as a human act, can employ the range of human emotion and ought to engage both the preacher's and the congregation's heart. But emotions can be misaimed. To preach with compassion, then, is to preach with a pervasive concern for the expansion of the glory of

Christ, a deep affection for the church, and a sincere and thorough desire for lost souls to be rescued from their sin.

## Is Your Sermon Cross-Centered?

This last question is perhaps the most important in all our preaching. We can preach an expository sermon with clarity and conviction and even compassion, but if we've missed the gospel of Jesus Christ, we've not preached a Christian sermon. We can even preach about Jesus without preaching Jesus. This occurs whenever we refer to Christ for quotable tidbits or as a moral exemplar—"Jesus was bold, so you be bold." These are fine turns to make. Jesus's quotes are the best! He really is our example, and we should strive to emulate him. But neither of these approaches reflects the good news. They are a preaching about Jesus without preaching Jesus.

Ask yourself this: Could this sermon be preached in a synagogue? A Mormon temple? A Jehovah's Witness kingdom hall? Each of these religions affirms the moral uplift of the Scriptures. Each of them uses the Bible to make inspirational, spiritual points about doing good to others and honoring God. But the one thing we have that they do not is the gospel. *It is the gospel that chiefly distinguishes Christian preaching from unchristian preaching.* Only the gospel of Christ's cross and resurrection can both save a lost soul and sanctify a found one. It is God's grace in the good news of Christ's life, death, and rising to glory that provides the power sinners need to grow and go, and it is only God's grace that does that.

This is why Paul resolved in his ministry "to know nothing . . . except Jesus Christ and him crucified" (1 Cor 2:2). I have chosen the phrase "cross-centered" from this resolution. I do not take Paul to mean he does not preach the resurrection or thinks the other aspects of Christ's work are unimportant. In 1 Corinthians 15, in fact, he defines the gospel by the cross and resurrection and goes on to explicate the glories of the latter. But for the apostles, "the cross" became a kind of shorthand for the gospel message. (Think of "the message of the cross is foolishness," for example, in 1 Corinthians 1:18.) And to get to the resurrection glory, we must go through the work of the cross.

Must the cross be mentioned in every sermon? Yes. We don't have to say the exact same thing about it. The beauty of Christ's atonement is that there are multiple glories there in which to revel. But the apostolic example is a carrying of the message of the cross. It is a reminder that our debt is canceled, our sin is pardoned, our judgment is taken, God's wrath is absorbed, and righteousness is accomplished. So, yes, *preach the cross as the center announcement in your sermon*. Don't just tack it on to the end as a completely unnatural addition to your sermon, disconnected from its textual trajectory. This communicates that the cross is incidental to Scripture and also to your sermon.

Remember that the good news of the cross is power (Rom 1:16; 1 Cor 1:18). The cross of Christ is the proof of God's great love for sinners. It certainly proves his immense, holy hatred of sin, but at the same time, it displays his deep, abounding, climactic love for sinners. The preacher's impulse to "get to the cross," in fact, is directly connected to his pastoral impulse for his flock. If you love the Lord, you will feed the sheep (John 21:15).

Contextual. Convictional. Clear. Compassionate. Cross-centered. Preaching can be lots of other things, but in order to satisfy the Bible's expectations for proclamation of itself and in order to supernaturally impact believers and unbelievers alike, preaching must nonnegotiably include those five characteristics.

## Preaching as a Pastoral Act

The preacher paced the stage, staring earnestly out into the congregation. It was time for his weekly invitation. He asked for respondents to raise their hands. Not a single hand was raised. But he had no way of knowing this because he was on a video screen.

I found myself at the nearest campus of this multisite church on assignment from the pastor himself, a man who had recently hired me to do some freelance research work for him. Visiting one of his many remote services was supposed to help me get a "feel" for his ministry. It certainly did. But I was struck right away with the notion that this way of doing ministry couldn't really help the preacher get a "feel" for his congregation.

Of course, it's impossible for a preacher of even a small congregation to be best friends with everybody in his church, and it's impossible for preachers of larger churches to know everybody well. But the preacher whose ministry is becoming more and more about preaching and less and less about shepherding, the preacher who is becoming less and less involved with his congregation, is actually undermining the task to which he is trying to devote more of his time! *Good preaching requires up-close shepherding.*

The ministry of preaching cannot be divorced from the ministry of soul care; in fact, preaching is actually an extension of soul care. Pastoring isn't preaching, but preaching *is* pastoring. There are a host of reasons why it is important for preachers to see their work as essentially pastoral, but the following are four of the most important:

## Pastoral Preaching Confronts Local Idols

As I travel to preach in church services and conferences, one of the first questions I usually ask the pastor who invited me is "What are your people's idols?" I don't just want to drop in and "do my thing" but to serve this pastor and his congregation by speaking to any of the hopes and dreams within the church that are not devotionally attached to Christ as their greatest satisfaction. Sadly, some pastors don't know how to answer the question.

When Paul walks into Athens, he sees that the city is full of idols (Acts 17:16). He doesn't simply regard this as a philosophical problem; it is a spiritual problem that grieves him personally. And when he addresses it, he does so specifically, referencing their devotion to "an unknown god" (17:23). And whenever Paul addresses specific churches in his letters, we see that the kinds of sins and falsehoods he identifies are very specific. He doesn't speak in generalizations. He knows what is going on in these churches. Paul's example doesn't mean, of course, that preachers should begin embarrassing or exposing people from the pulpit. But it does mean that we are in the thick of congregational life enough to speak in familiar terms.

Until a pastor has spent quality time with people in his congregation, the idols his preaching must combat with the gospel will be merely theoretical. All human beings have a few universal idols in common. But communities where churches are located, congregations as a subculture themselves, and even specific cliques and demographics within congregations tend to traffic in more specific idols and patterns of sin. Knowing firsthand your flock's misguided financial, career, and familial hopes will help you know how to preach. It will help you pick the right texts and the right emphases in explicating those texts. This is what makes preaching a ministry and not simply an exercise.

## Pastoral Preaching Is Empathetic

My preaching changed after I'd begun holding people's hands while they died and hearing people's hearts while they cried. Until you've heard enough people share their sins and fears and worries and wounds, your preaching can be excellent and passionate, but it will not be all that it can be. It will not be resonant.

Preach with authority and conviction—because the Word of God stands over us—but preach with a heart that is *with* your people, *for* them, a heart that is set alongside every other heart in the pews below.

Many preachers carry the burden of God's Word into the pulpit, and this is a good thing. Receiving the heavy mantle of preaching hot with Christ's glory and being burdened to proclaim the Lord's favor in the gospel is a noble, worthy, and wonderful task. But the preacher must also feel the weight of his people's burdens in that pulpit. We must ascend to preach, having been in the valley with them. Our manuscripts should be smudged with the tears of our people.

Knowing what sufferings afflict our people on a regular basis will keep us from becoming tone-deaf to our congregations. We won't be lighthearted in the wrong places. It will affect the kinds of illustrations we use, the types of stories we tell, and—most importantly—the disposition with which we handle the Bible. I have seen preachers make jokes about things people in their congregations were actually struggling with, and I've been that preacher. We come to lift burdens, but with careless words we sometimes end up adding to them.

Preacher, do you have a genuine heart for your people? I don't mean "Are you a people person?" I mean, do you know what is going on in the lives of your congregation, and does it move you, grieve you? Have you wept with those who weep? If not, over time your preaching will show it.

Think of Moses's grief over his people's sins (Exod 32:32). Or of Paul's abundant tears (Acts 20:31; 2 Cor 2:4; Phil 3:18; 2 Tim 1:4). Think, also, of Christ's compassion, seeing into the hearts of the people (Matt 9:36). You may believe you can work these feelings up without really knowing your congregation; but it isn't the same for them in the same way that hearing a stirring word from a role model is not the same as hearing a stirring word from your dad. Preacher, don't take to your text without carrying the real burdens of your people in your heart.

## Pastoral Preaching Has Names in Mind

Every faithful preacher prays over his sermon. He prays that God's Word will not return void (Isa 55:11). He prays that people will be receptive. He prays that souls will be saved and lives will be changed. These are good prayers. Better still is the sermon prepped and composed with prayers for John Smith and Julie Thompson and the Cunningham family on the lips of the preacher. Better still is the sermon prayed over in pleadings for Tom Johnson's salvation and Bill Lewis's repentance and Mary Alice's healing.

Paul repeatedly tells the people under his care that he is remembering them in his prayers (Eph 1:16; 2 Tim 1:3; Phlm 4). And since he is frequently naming names, we know he doesn't just mean generally. And while Paul did not have just one congregation to shepherd up close but served largely as a missionary church planter, he nevertheless worked hard to know the people he ministered to from a distance and sought to visit them as often as he could. How much more should the local church pastor develop relationships with his people! He should know their names and he should carry their names to heaven in prayer.

Knowing to whom you're preaching is important. It's important to know that Sister Squinty-Eye doesn't like your preaching. It's important to know that Brother Puff-You-Up likes it too much. It's important to know that the man in the back with his arms folded and his brow furrowed isn't actually angry—that's just how he listens. It's important to know that the smiling, nodding lady near the front has a tendency to forget everything you've said. When you know these things, you can pray for your people in deeper, more personal, more pastoral ways. And your preaching will get better. It will be more real. It will come not just from your mind and mouth, but from your heart, your soul, and your guts.

## Pastoral Preaching Is the Fruit of Real Labor

Because preaching is a work of love and conviction, we must take care to do the work ourselves. We cannot outsource love and conviction. Therefore, I'd like to say a word about the strange phenomenon of pastoral plagiarism. It is reaching epidemic levels in the evangelical church and is increasingly excused or even defended. There are men out there, perhaps even some reading this book, who have made a practice of taking other people's sermons and passing them off as their own. There are numerous reasons why this should be avoided and repented of.

First, and perhaps most importantly, it is dishonest. Misrepresenting someone else's words as your own is a form of lying. How can you expect to commend the truth to others while you convey a lie?

Secondly, the model preacher whose work you are plagiarizing does not know your congregation's needs. And he doesn't know your congregation. No one knows them like you do. You are shortchanging your people—failing to love them—by feeding them someone else's leftovers instead of the fruit of your own labor.

Thirdly, since "able to teach" is one of the qualifications for the pastorate, the preacher who is merely replicating the teaching of others, treating the sermon as a kind of performance of another's music, is bringing his credibility as a pastor into question. Unrepentant pastoral plagiarism is, in fact, disqualifying for ministry.

Finally, plagiarism is a shortcut to the fruit you want. It reveals a distrust in God's gifts to you and, further, a distrust in the gospel. It is not someone's eloquence or well-spun stories that will change people; it is the good news of Jesus. No one can improve on that. You may not be as good a preacher as the author of your stolen sermons, but they can't preach a gospel that is any more glorious than the one you've already got. Lean into it. Work hard throughout the week. Study and pray. Dig into the text and into your heart. Bring the meager work of your own hands into that pulpit each week, and by God's grace, exult in Christ's excellencies. You will eventually see the fruit of your real labor, not poached goods from another's.

Yes, preaching is hard. Yes, weekly sermon prep can be a slog, particularly if you feel overburdened to always find new, creative, or inventive things. But, even without these excessive external expectations, the regular work of exegetically excavating the Word to expositionally proclaim it still requires a resolute commitment to press on. It is "through endurance and through the encouragement of the Scriptures" that "we might have hope" (Rom 15:4 ESV).

## Preaching as an Expository Act

The resurgence in commitment to expository preaching in many evangelical circles is a very encouraging sign as the contemporary church navigates shifting cultural trends and its own shifting stylistic trends. Many younger churchmen have begun to look not at the latest preaching styles but at what evangelicalism's elder statesmen have been doing for years. More than this, they've begun studying the homiletical practices of the gospel renewal movements throughout church history. A fortunate result of this is a rise in expositional preaching.

Many of us have maintained a commitment to this kind of explication, even when our sermons happen to be topical. There's no need to be dogmatic about this kind of sermon delivery, and I think taking time for short topical sermon series or strategic "stand-alone" messages can be good and helpful. However, I do think it is generally wise for a pastor not just to preach individual sermons expositionally but to preach expositionally through entire books of the Bible—what I call "enduring exposition" (because it is regular exposition that endures through the preaching of the Word). This has been the traditional form of expositional preaching throughout church history, and I am fond of recovering the practice. Every preacher ought to endeavor to feed his flock this way, and here are eight reasons why:

### Enduring Exposition Is Thoroughly Biblical

Expository preaching through books of the Bible has biblical precedent, contrary to the claims of some. We can see in texts previously mentioned; in Nehemiah 8, where Ezra and the scribes preached through the book of the Law, "giving the sense" (v. 8 ESV) as they go; and of course in Luke 24, where "beginning with Moses and all the Prophets, [Jesus] interpreted to them in all the Scriptures the things concerning himself" (v. 27 ESV). There is biblical precedent for following the story line of an entire book in preaching.

## Enduring Exposition Helps People Learn Their Bible

The truth is, the most Bible most of our people will get each week will occur on Sunday morning. We wish that weren't true, but it is. We want them to spend daily time in the Word, of course, but too many don't and won't. Preaching through books of the Bible, then, over time, exposes churchgoers to the fullness of God's counsel. This is even true for Christians who do study their Bibles, but who tend to do so like their preachers tend to preach, favoring certain books or stories or devotional emphases. If a preacher will preach through whole books, he will eventually get to more "obscure" books, in which even some studious Christians haven't yet spent much time.

## Enduring Exposition Spiritually Stretches the Preacher and Deepens His Understanding of God

If preachers will commit to preaching through entire books of the Bible, we will find ourselves dealing with difficult and complex passages we might otherwise have avoided. Systematically working through a book means we can't skip the confusing parts or the scandalous parts or the "boring" parts. Since *all* Scripture is breathed out by God and useful (2 Tim 3:16), the study of all of it is helpful to the preacher's own devotional life and consequently helpful to the congregation.

## Enduring Exposition Puts Controversial or "Hot Topic" Issues in Their Proper Place

A preacher committed to preaching through books of the Bible can't hobbyhorse or camp out on one political, social, or cultural issue he feels most important. His preaching isn't driven by Hallmark or the headlines. Thus, he gets around to the "social issues" when the Bible does and ends up correlating his concern and energy about them to the Bible's concern and energy about them.

## Enduring Exposition Helps Christians See the Full Story Line of Redemption

The gospel announcement of Christ's sinless life, sacrificial death, and glorious resurrection for the salvation of sinners is a grand plan foreshadowed and echoed throughout all of Scripture; preaching through entire books of the Bible helps churches see the epic story God is telling about his Son from the foundation of the world. Which leads us to the next point. . . .

## Enduring Exposition More Greatly Magnifies the Glory of Jesus Christ

As Jesus himself says to those disciples on the road to Emmaus, even the old covenant Scriptures are "about himself" (Luke 24:27). And as Paul says, all the promises of God find their "yes" and "amen" in Jesus (2 Cor 1:20). Failing to preach through as many biblical texts as we can is to withhold certain aspects of Christ's glory from our churches. To preach systematically through books of the Bible—laboring faithfully in the work of *Christ-centered* exposition—is to show the glory of Christ in surprising, fresh, and God-designed ways.

## Enduring Exposition Fosters Congregational Endurance

Hopping from one topic to the next, jumping around according to pastoral interest or current devotional mood, has some advantages to be sure, but a commitment to a book more befits the plodding needed for faithful long-term ministry. Preachers who preach through books of the Bible logically think in more long-term ways, which is beneficial for pastoral fruitfulness. And the way preachers preach shapes their churches. A pastor who commits to showing Christ week after week through book after book rewires the short attention spans of modern congregants to the Spiritual fruit of patience, the Christian virtue of endurance, and the church's mandate to be "people of the book." Nothing shows a pastor's and a congregation's fidelity to and reliance on the Word of God alone like preaching all of it exclusively.

## Enduring Exposition Creates a Longer Pastoral and Congregational Legacy

C. S. Lewis once said, "To move with the times is, of course, to go where all times go."[1] Similarly, to preach with the times is to see our preaching legacy fade away. Now, sermons ought to be applicable and relevant to the Christian's daily life and the world in which we live. But the great thing about the Scriptures is that they are remarkably applicable and relevant to the world we live in without our help! And while sermons fashioned toward the tyranny of the now may be of some help for some time, sermons preached from the eternal Word can be of help for all time. In the long run of pastoral ministry and the life of the church, a pastor who resources his congregation with faithful, plodding biblical exposition is providing a body of work that will live long after his own departure.

What a milestone it would be to get to the end of preaching through the entire New Testament to your church or even, should God grant you this length of tenure, the entire Bible! Wouldn't that be a finish line worth shooting for?

And yet each week brings a finish line of its own. Some pastors are just angling to get through to Sunday and preach that sermon. And then it's over. Everyone goes home. And Monday morning there's a blank page facing you, yet again. What do you do with that? In such moments, spiritually speaking, the most important preaching may be the kind you do to yourself. Remind yourself daily of

---

1. C.S. Lewis, "Period Criticism," in *"On Stories" and Other Essays on Literature* (Orlando, FL: Harcourt, 1982), 115.

the goodness of God in the gospel—that your approval before God is not based on your performance or your eloquence, your ability to "hit one out of the park," and so forth. Preach the gospel well to yourself, and then you will be on your way to preaching the needed grace to your flock.

Practically speaking, then, there is quite a bit that goes into turning that blank page into a vehicle for the glory of Christ. And it is to the more practical side of preaching that I will turn next.

## For Reflection

1. How would you distinguish preaching from teaching?
2. What was the best sermon you ever heard? What made it so impressive to you?
3. In which of the "five Cs" of preaching do you think you need the most development? Why?
4. What can go wrong if we separate the practice of preaching from the context of *pastoring*?
5. What message must be included in every sermon? Why?

## For Further Study:

Clowney, Edmund P. *Preaching Christ in All of Scripture.* Wheaton, IL: Crossway, 2003.

Few scholars have helped preachers see the logical necessity of preaching Christ from every text in order to have constructed a Christian sermon like Westminster's Clowney.

Fuller, Andrew. *Preaching.* Peterborough, Ontario: H&E, 2018.

The Baptist missionary Fuller is not exactly well-known today for his preaching ministry, but this book, built around letters of advice to a young minister, is outstanding for its repeated emphasis on gospel-centrality.

Grimké, Francis James. *Meditations on Preaching.* Madison, MS: Log College Press, 2018.

Organized as a series of "proverbial" excerpts, à la Pascal's *Pensées*, this short work from the rich mind of an African American preacher is full of gospel goodness.

# CHAPTER 5

# PREACHING *Part 2*

It was one of the worst ideas I've ever had. But I sure thought I was clever.

I decided I was going to preach my entire sermon one Sunday morning while wandering the congregation and washing people's feet. Now, my first instinct was to think that it would not be good to surprise people with this act of intimacy, especially in a public setting. So, I spent some time calling some men in the church and asking if I could wash their feet come Sunday. To my surprise, they all said yes. Not to my surprise, they each showed up with the cleanest feet they'd ever had in their lives. I would only be washing prewashed feet that morning.

What I hadn't expected was the anxiety in the rest of the congregation. They didn't know I had made arrangements with these men ahead of time. All they saw was the pastor roaming the pews with a water basin and towel, washing feet. For all they knew, they might be next. You could cut the tension in the sanctuary with a knife.

My sermon text that day was *the entire Old Testament*. I had had the clever idea of washing feet while extemporaneously working through the major plot points of the Old Testament—highlighting God's presence with his people—building up to the climactic miracle of the Incarnation, when the God of the universe came as a suffering servant.

In my head, it was going to go great.

I don't think anybody heard a word I said. The spectacle and the worry were too much. But it was just as well. I rambled. I fumbled. Multitasking is not my strong suit, and trying to maintain a clear, coherent train of thought—much less an exposition of the Scriptures— while washing feet proved incredibly difficult. I remembered in the midst of it why I had switched from outline preaching to manuscript preaching a few years prior. What made me think I could pull this off extemporaneously? Pride. Pure and simple. I let my good idea get in the way of what I knew about myself (and God's Word), and the gimmick of the thing eclipsed the goodness of preaching.

There are several reasons why this exercise was a failure. Some of them are related to a poor philosophy of preaching, others to the overlooked practicalities of preaching. Pastors must remain mindful of both. The gospel-driven pastor isn't simply seeking to explicate grace in his content. We want to employ grace in our work, our organization, our construction. It is *all* an act of love (or should be), and we are not pragmatists for seeking to think through the "nuts and bolts" of sermon construction and delivery.

## Preparing the Sermon

The place to begin is always with a text. Even if you're preaching a topical sermon, preach a text. You may say that no one text says all you'd like to say on a given topic, but that is okay. No one sermon can say everything there is to say on a given topic either. Remember that a sermon is not a commentary. In any event, if you select a text from which to carry out your exposition, you can always bring in other texts that give your hearers a sense of the wider counsel of Scripture on that topic. But whether you are preaching through a book of the Bible or a topical series, begin your preparation with a text.

## Steep in the Text

The text will set the agenda. Let ideas from the text arise naturally through your study of that text. *Let God's words shape yours.*

Start as early as you are able. Some pastors like to begin the work of a sermon several weeks out. For most of us, this is simply not feasible. Pastors of normative-size churches have their weeks full already with ecclesial and familial obligations. So, don't be discouraged or envious of the pastor who is always weeks ahead in sermon prep. It is normal to be scraping up the sheep's feed week to week.

What is not normal or commendable is waiting until the end of the week to begin your sermon preparation in earnest. If the bulk of your work must take place on Saturday evenings, so be it. But avoid beginning your work on Saturday night. The result of Saturday night sermons is typically Sunday morning confusion. You need to give yourself time to steep in the Word.

At my last pastorate, I made a regular Monday routine of printing out my upcoming sermon text and keeping the page under my nose on my desk. (I scheduled my preaching texts months in advance, but still conducted sermon prep week to week.) The bulk of my sermon prep did not commence until Wednesday, but for two days prior I took time to stare at that page, prayerfully meditating on the passage, jotting little notes and questions on the page. I didn't dive in until Wednesday, but I was wetting my feet in it Monday and Tuesday. This helped immensely because, by Sunday, it meant I had spent an entire week rolling the text around in my mind and heart. I gave myself time to be challenged and formed by the passage. This makes for better preaching.

## Find the "Big Idea"

Everyone's exegetical process is different; find what works for you. But generally, the first thing you'll need to do is make sense of the text's meaning. What, in general, is the passage saying? It may be saying several things. Can you find an overarching summation of those messages? Can you organize the messages under a concluding headline? A few readings of the text should yield to you some sense of the big idea.

What you are basically doing is putting your "ability to teach" to the test. You are leaning on your gift to teach, as well as your doctrinal soundness, your spiritual wisdom, and your experiential knowledge of God and the Bible in general. All of these are brought to bear as you determine the "big idea"—a simple statement that captures the text's major theme, primary message, or central problem.

## Compose an Exegetical Outline

Once you have a sense of the big idea, you can begin forming an exegetical outline. This will become the skeleton of your understanding of the text and become the template for your eventual sermon outline. The exegetical outline consists of the primary plot movements or data points from the text that support the big idea. You may have numerous points in your exegetical outline, but it is wise to limit yourself to three or four, perhaps five. Rarely should your exegetical outline consist of more than five points; that usually translates into an information-glutted sermon that will become too long or too complicated for your audience to follow. (Remember that clarity is a hallmark of Christian preaching.)

It is important to compose your exegetical outline and other words of preliminary exposition before you begin consulting secondary sources like commentaries. The reasons for this are twofold. First, you are working *your* gift to teach, not someone else's. Every week, the weight of interpretation is on you, the pastor. Obviously, some passages are more difficult to adequately grasp than others; but if you find that you are struggling week to week to make sense of a text without help, there is either a qualification problem or a spiritual problem at work. Second, by putting off consultation of others' work until a later stage, you are more likely to borrow than to steal. What I mean is, you will find others' insights either complementary or challenging to your own, rather than allowing their exposition or explication to set the agenda for yours.

Now you have your exegetical outline, which represents your own basic understanding of the text. You have the big idea, and now also a set of supporting ideas for it. As in English composition, it is like devising a thesis statement about a given literary work and then finding evidential "substatements" to prove your thesis. The next step is to consult your commentaries and other reference works.

## Consult Secondary Sources

It is wise to limit your use of secondary sources. Too much input can overload your own sense of clarity and divert the straightforwardness of your exposition. The sermon is not your opportunity to follow every theological rabbit trail and go down every linguistic rabbit hole. Employ enough voices that you get a good chorus of wisdom to draw from, a well-rounded consultation, but not so many that you end up composing a research paper more than preparing a sermon.

It is important not to get stuck in the rut of the same voices each week, but of course some reference works have become standards because of their long-proven reliability and the beauty of their insights. I think of the works of the Reformers and Puritans in particular, but also of many of the church fathers. Nevertheless, ask others what references have helped them. Appeal to appropriate diversity. Don't be afraid of one or two works outside your own tradition.

Modern technical commentaries can be helpful, especially for preachers who work from the original languages, but be discerning about how much of this work you let bleed into your exposition. Technical works can help the exegete get a handle on the text's depth and complexity, but they are typically not aimed at laypeople or general congregations. Thus, technical commentaries are more helpful for the initial working out of tricky translations and other exegetical dead ends in the pastor's study than they are for helping congregations in the Sunday morning sanctuary.

Consult a few homiletical commentaries or other expositional reference sources to "check your work." It's possible your exegetical outline may need tweaking. It's possible it will need revising. But it's also possible you will find some of your favorite scholars and preachers sharing the same grasp of the text as you. This can be extremely rewarding. To discover that Martin Luther had the same view as your own on that tricky spot in Galatians 3? What joy!

## Refine Your Work

With your exegetical outline and the initial sputtering of exposition, you have now consulted secondary sources to "check your work." You have seen some of your primary thoughts confirmed and others challenged. You have also discovered insights you did not anticipate. With all of that information, you are now able to begin refining both your outline and your exposition. Other voices have added their weight to the process in which you have already done much of the heavy lifting, and your understanding of the text—and how it might be preached—is becoming clearer and clearer.

Refining may also include consultation from your fellow pastors, friends, members of the congregation, or members of your family. Their perception of the "big idea" of the passage may influence yours. Their understanding of the exegetical components of the passage may challenge (or confirm) your own.

As you further refine your grasp of the text itself—what it means—you may find yourself rewriting certain points or adjusting your articulation of the big idea. The goal is to revisit your understanding of the text enough times that it feels familiar to you but still fresh.

At this point you may already be thinking of illustrations, other points of thematic entry and exit for the sermon, introductory thoughts or questions, and concluding applications or exhortations. All of this should go down in your preparation record, but do not run too far just yet. Before you compose your exposition in full, it is time to translate your exegetical outline into a homiletical outline.

## Compose a Homiletical Outline

At this point in the process, you will create the outline you will use in your actual sermon. The points of your homiletical outline are basically your "sermon points," the things you share with your audience. (Maybe you also put them on a screen or print them in a bulletin.)

How does the homiletical outline differ from the exegetical outline? For starters, the exegetical outline is essentially a skeleton of data, the plot points or movements in a text's argument. The homiletical outline is much more refined. While the points of your exegetical outline can be expressed in lengthy sentences, none of which resemble the other in form, the homiletical outline should be composed of points that are as succinct and clear as possible and that also share a kind of symmetry in form. Many preachers here have traditionally used alliteration or acronyms. I don't think this is entirely necessary, and at times it can approach a kitschy kind of cleverness that actually distracts from the primary point of the whole sermon.

But thoughtful symmetry in the homiletical outline is a good way to begin thinking through the clarity and conviction of your sermon. Clarity, because you want your audience to be able to track with your message. This is the primary purpose, in fact, of sermon points and the reason there shouldn't be too many. (I think three or four is almost always the right amount.) The sermon points serve as handholds, like rungs on a ladder for the congregation to work through the sermon with you. The sad fact is that most congregants will not remember your sermon points by the following week. Most will forget by Sunday afternoon. And this is okay. The points aren't primarily to deliver memorable phrasing but to provide in-the-moment clarity about the text and the big idea. You want the most memorable thing to be the gospel and its connection to the text in question.

Symmetry in your message points helps with making sure your preaching is convictional, as well, because it entails translating the data points of good exegesis into the declaration of good homiletics. Your homiletical outline should consist of points that are proclamational, not merely propositional. They should be assertions (from the text) drawn directly from your exegetical outline that in some way "announce" truth.

Below is an example of how I've translated an exegetical outline of Titus 2:11–15 to a homiletical outline. First the passage itself:

> For the grace of God has appeared, bringing salvation for all people, training us to renounce ungodliness and worldly passions, and to live self-controlled, upright, and godly lives in the present age, waiting for our blessed hope, the appearing of the glory of our great God and Savior Jesus Christ, who gave himself for us to redeem us from all lawlessness and to purify for himself a people for his own possession who are zealous for good works.
>
> Declare these things; exhort and rebuke with all authority. Let no one disregard you. (ESV)

I settled on this statement as the big idea for the text:

> Grace has come in the person of Jesus, and he is coming again, so we must behave accordingly.

This thematic statement became this title for my sermon: "Living This Time in Light of That Time."

Here is my exegetical outline supporting the big idea, including verse references to show my source for each statement:

1. Paul names grace—which is embodied in Jesus—as the source of power to change. (vv. 11–12)
2. Paul references waiting for the hope of Jesus, who will consummate this change. (v. 13)
3. Paul says in the meantime, we have been redeemed to bear witness through good works. (vv. 14–15)

Eventually, my exegetical outline was reformulated into the following homiletical outline. These are the actual preaching points of my sermon:

1. The gospel is our only power.
2. Christ is our only hope.
3. Redemption is our only vision.

Notice the symmetry of the points. Each is expressed as "Noun is our only noun."

## Complete Your Exposition and Compose Your Sermon

Now that you have your homiletical outline (your sermon points), you are ready to begin filling in the gaps between them with your exposition of the text. This consists primarily of showing how the text gives rise to each point and then amplifying that proclamation by means of declaration, illustration, and application.

The declaration is the most important part of the exposition. It is the substance of your preaching the word. It is "giving the meaning" (Neh 8:8).

Illustrations help people visualize the declaration or take it to heart. They can also help explain the declaration. (I will say more about illustrations shortly.)

Application is how you exhort people to respond to the declaration. This can be done throughout the sermon in little ways. Application is best derived directly from any imperatives in the text. It's important to say that gospel-centrality does not mean imperative-denial. We want to keep the commands of Scripture (law) in the context of the announcements of Scripture (gospel), but we don't need to avoid, spin, or dismiss them. And yet, if the text is devoid of imperatives, be circumspect about the prospect of smuggling them in.

Some preachers will tell you that any sermon without application is not a sermon at all. This depends on what they mean by application. Typically, what is meant is a list of practical steps—physical "things to do." In this case, I wholeheartedly disagree—not every message will lend itself to the demand for such steps. We have few examples of this "requirement" in biblical preaching, for one thing. For another, it tends to betray a misunderstanding of the law/gospel dynamic.

But there is more than one way to apply the Word of God. Biblically speaking, the most common application point in any sermon is "repent and believe" (Mark 1:15; Acts 2:37–38). That is certainly something to do, but not in the way most emphasizers of application usually mean it. Keep in mind that faithful application can also consist of things to think, things to confess, and even things to feel.

In summary, the process of sermon preparation may look like this:

Text
Meditation/exegesis
Exegetical outline
Secondary sources
Refinement
Homiletical outline
Detailed sermon outline or manuscript

## A Case for Sermon Manuscripting

When the preparation is done, the work of delivery remains. One important aspect of delivery is how many notes the preacher uses during the sermon. It is unnecessary to be dogmatic about what material a preacher takes into the pulpit or what that material should look like on the page (or tablet). Some preachers can capably carry out their sermon with very little material, if any at all. Others of us rely on full manuscripts. Find what works for you over time.

I am quite fond of manuscripting for a few reasons. One, it keeps me on track. I am never at a loss as to what to say. I never forget how to transition from one point to another. I've thought it all out beforehand and written it down. I simply need to follow the tracks I laid down for myself.

Second, I have come to know how many pages roughly equates to my desired timeframe for preaching, and it is rare that I preach much longer (or shorter) than expected. Manuscripting prevents time-consuming, spur-of-the-moment rabbit trails.

Thirdly, composing a manuscript produces a complete resource that can be better used later. Most of us record our preaching today, and congregants can always consult that video or audio. But many appreciate a written, word-for-word record of the message. Similarly, for those of us who write online or for print, manuscripts are more easily transitioned into other written resources that bless others. You could always re-create your thoughts after the fact, but why add the extra work?

Finally, my sermon delivery is much more polished. Preaching from a manuscript has virtually eliminated the "um"s and "uh"s to which I am inclined in extemporaneous speech. I am a better preacher from a full manuscript than I'd be without one.

Maybe you are different. But I fear many beginning preachers give up on manuscripting too soon, before they've really grown accustomed to it. As with most difficult things, it takes a long practice to get better. Certainly, if preaching from a manuscript, over time, is sounding like a rote reading rather than a passionate preaching, perhaps preaching from a manuscript is not for you. But don't give up before you've dedicated time to get better at it. Be aware of eye contact with your audience, your posture in the pulpit, your tone of voice, your hand gestures, and the like. These all help someone preaching from a manuscript offer a delivery that doesn't look or sound like someone simply reading.

## The Substance of Your Outline

A good homiletical outline is organized both for ease of the preacher's communication and ease of the hearer's understanding. Think of the outline as a set of stairs, each step a progression toward the destination (or conclusion). I like to think of my sermon points as rungs on a ladder, in fact, that give the audience something to "grasp" as they progress through the sermon with me.

The less organized your outline, the more confusing and perhaps even rambling your sermon may be. Clear organization makes for clearer communication.

Below is a sample template for a sermon outline. This is the basic template that I use personally in my own sermon composition. I occasionally stray from this template but only rarely. I have found it a sturdy skeleton for the meat of my manuscripting.

> Thematic Intro
> Whole Text
> "This is the word of the Lord" / Pray
> Formal Intro
> Point 1
> > Verse(s)
> > Exposition
> > Illustration
> Point 2
> > Verse(s)
> > Exposition
> > Illustration

Point 3
    Verse(s)
    Exposition
    Illustration
Conclusion/invitation

Let me offer a few words of explanation regarding this outline.

The thematic introduction is how I set up the problem or subject the sermon will be addressing. I may use a kind of illustration here, but it is not likely to be a very lengthy one. Some preachers begin their sermons with a story. I share their affinity for thematic introductions but often find that starting with a story overly delays getting to the text. In effect, the story ends up setting the agenda. If I tell a story, it will be a short one, more of an anecdote. The point of the thematic introduction is to get people on your train of thought toward the "big idea," if not presenting the big idea outright.

After the thematic introduction, I read the whole passage without interruption. If my preaching text is only a couple of verses, I may read the longer context. I want to present the text at the front as a means of communicating that all I say is meant to be derived from *this* authority, from *this* declaration. I am fond of the traditional refrain "This is the Word of the Lord" after the Scripture reading (and I am warmed in nonliturgical church settings when I hear a smattering of "Thanks be to God"s from the congregation). This is my way of joining with the historic church in setting apart God's words as essentially different from my own.

I usually offer a short pastoral prayer after the Scripture reading, asking the Lord to bless the preaching of his Word and interceding for the congregation. I typically also ask our Father to show us all a glimpse of the glory of Jesus, as I want to acknowledge to him and also to the public hearers that none of us can be changed without it.

The sermon begins in earnest with a more formal introduction, and it is here that I will set the context or circumstance of the biblical text. Who is the audience? When was this written? What is the point of the book from which the text is pulled? If I am in a series, I may do this by way of reminder about the previous messages and "what we've learned so far." If it is a stand-alone message, I just want my hearers to get a sense of the purpose of the source material. From this, I will transition by connecting that context to the big idea. It could sound like this: "Paul's concern in Galatians is primarily about the reiteration of justification by grace through faith as opposed to self-righteous works . . . which is why his word for us today in Galatians 2:20 about being crucified with Christ is so important to hear."

There's no one way to do this, but I have learned that transitional statements are often the most difficult feature of a sermon for many preachers to pull off. They don't know how to start, end, or connect all the joints. Dedicate ample time to thinking over how each of your points fits together, how to move excellently from one section to another. How does *this thing* you just said give way to this thing you're *about* to say?

From here, we move into the part of the sermon that should take most of your time—the homiletical outline and the exposition filling it out. My sample above shows three points but could easily be expanded (or shortened). Again, keep in mind that most people won't remember your sermon points. Yes, even if you use alliteration, even if the first letter of each point spells a word, even if they are clever or poignant or "powerful."

Oh sure, every now and again a certain point or two may strike a certain hearer as a particularly fresh word from the Lord. I remember exactly one point from all of my pastor's sermons during my middle school years—"You have to squash the spider, not just wipe away the web." It struck me then and I still remember it today because at the time, like most young men, I was struggling with lustful thoughts and the temptations of sexually provocative images.

I took this word as a conviction from the Spirit, a mandate to become more intentional in my fight against the flesh.

But the vast majority of your message points will not have a very wide impact at all. Again, the points of your sermon are best thought of not as permanent reminders but as temporary handholds through the sermon. They help explicate the meaning of the text, yes. They are vitally important truths about the ultimate truth of God's Word, yes. But they mainly serve to help people in the moment understand the Word and "track" through your message.

This is why it is not advisable to employ too many points in your outline. It is the rare preacher who can sustain concentrated interest and understanding beyond four or five points. Each extraneous point deducts importance from each of the others. You compound forgetfulness when you give too much information.

When you come to the end of your final point, you will want to transition into a thoughtful conclusion. Too many sermons end very abruptly, as if the preacher is always running out of time, as if a trapdoor is about to open up beneath him. Rhetorically, this often feels like a kind of whiplash or crashing into an unseen wall. Don't belabor your conclusions, but think them through well. Conduct appropriate application, preferably drawn from the text or at least complementary to the text. Some pastors end their sermons with a list of application points, and the effect is that another sermon, even if shorter, is tacked on to the first. Another set of points, another bit of exposition can feel jarring. Worse, to end your messages frequently with a weighted list of dos and don'ts is a great way to send people home with the prevailing thought of what they ought to do for Jesus rather than what Jesus has done for them (which provides the actual power to live obediently)!

I have listed "invitation" at the end not because I am given to public altar calls—though I am not entirely opposed to them—but because biblical preaching does entail calling for people to repent and believe. Ideally, you are working this into the substance of your message all along. Saving it always for the end can feel like an arbitrary transition is being made. Regardless, don't be shy of a final exhortation to your congregation. Invite them to repent, to believe, to rejoice, to enter into the work that God is doing in the world and that can be theirs in Christ.

## Be Careful with Sermon Illustrations

In the last chapter, I mentioned that I used to do freelance research work for a pastor at a multisite church. Eventually, that pastor only wanted my help in generating sermon illustration ideas. It became my job to scour the gamut of lived experience to mine as many homiletical gems as possible. Over the course of several months, I filed numerous research briefs full of newspaper clippings, movie anecdotes, literary references, assorted fragments of pop culture detritus, and even some original creative stories. I think he eventually used about one illustration from each one of those briefs. Clearly, he thought sermon illustrations were crucially important! I've heard the same from numerous other preachers. They say the illustrations you choose can make or break your message.

We all know a good illustration when we hear one in a sermon, but I am of the somewhat firm opinion that sermon illustrations are typically far overrated. I think, in how we train preachers and in too many actual sermons, too much emphasis is put on illustrations. *You shouldn't trust your illustration to do what only God's Word can do.* And that's where many of us often go wrong with illustrations. The following cautions are intended to help you keep illustrations in their proper place.

### Beware of Illustrations That Are Too Long

If you're going to eat up valuable sermon time, make it really count. Some sermons are too reliant on long setups or overly developed creative themes that end up obscuring the biblical message. This is a problem, assuming that what you want people to focus on most is the biblical message. Some preachers really pride themselves in being storytellers or artists, and that's great if you haven't been called to be a minister of the gospel first and foremost. Storytelling and other forms of artistry certainly glorify God, but the point of preaching is not personal artistry. Some illustrations go on so long and some topic themes are so pervasive that any Bible verses that show up in the sermon really only serve to support the illustration. Do not preach an illustration in search of a text.

## Beware of Using Too Many Illustrations

I heard a message once that began with a 5-minute story from the preacher's childhood, segued into an anecdote from the life of Leonardo da Vinci, transitioned into a series of quotes from ancient philosophers (where Jesus took an undistinguished place alongside Socrates and Aristotle, as if they were all equal visages on a philosophical Mount Rushmore), and then stumbled into a heavy-handed object illustration complete with big props on the stage. This fellow forgot what he was there to do. The result of all these illustrations was distracting and actually counterproductive because, at some point, the law of diminishing illustration returns kicked in, and each successive illustration diminished the effectiveness of the ones before it.

When you use too many illustrations, when your sermon is so full of illustrations or the time you spend on them is greater than the time you spend proclaiming and explaining the text, they stop being illustrations and *become* your text. Preachers who overuse illustrations are communicating that they don't actually trust the Bible to be interesting, provocative, and powerful.

## Beware of Illustrations That Are Awkward

You know these when you hear them. Some illustrations are just unnatural; it seems as though the preacher prepared his sermon using some resource for illustrations rather than coming up with them naturally through his work in the text. Maybe he's plopped in something from an illustration book or website. Other illustrations are clunky. For example, the pop culture references are old, making the preacher seem hopelessly "out of touch." Maybe his stories are sappy. Or maybe there's no decent transition from the illustration into the body of the sermon. If the weight of power is put on your illustrations instead of the biblical text, an awkward illustration makes an ineffective sermon.

## Beware of Being Too Self-Referential

Many illustrations fail because they communicate a self-absorption that is a turn-off for hearers and a contradiction of the biblical message. Here's a good rule of thumb: when using yourself as an example, be self-deprecating. Make it confessional, not exaltational. In other words, use your personal illustrations to tell your audience not how great you are, but what you've gotten wrong, how you messed up, and where you're deficient. It doesn't have to be a serious example; it can be a funny one. But self-referential illustrations that talk up the preacher too often violate 2 Corinthians 4:5, "For what we proclaim is not ourselves. . . ."

This same rule applies somewhat to the use of wives and children in illustrations. Everyone appreciates a good story that demonstrates that the pastor is a normal guy with a normal family, and most preachers know not to criticize or point out flaws in their family members in sermons. But if you reference your wife and kids (even positively) too much, over time it can have the same effect as the self-congratulating illustration. It casts a vision of your family as the church's moral exemplar, which is not good for your family or the church, and also only serves to exalt yourself by extension. Use family illustrations sparingly (ideally, with the consent of the family member being referenced), and when using personal illustrations, go the route of self-deprecation.

Good illustrations can, indeed, be difficult to discover. Even the best preachers struggle with their proper use. But let's be as careful with how we use them. Remember that the hearts of people are not won to Christ by our well-spun stories or images, but by the Spirit working through the very Word of God. Our illustrations are meant to adorn the gospel, not help it. The gospel doesn't need any help.

## Officiating Weddings

The pastor engaged in the week in, week out work of expositional preaching may find his rhythm disrupted by the request for preaching at ceremonial occasions. Are the compositional requirements for these messages the same as those for a Sunday sermon? How should the pastor think about his involvement in a wedding ceremony, for instance?

Before you have the blessing of being asked to officiate a marriage ceremony, you should make clear to yourself your convictions on the issues of marriage, divorce, remarriage, and the like. Will you officiate weddings involving unbelievers? Will you only officiate weddings involving people you know personally? Must the prospective husband and wife meet with you for premarital counseling?

Once you've determined your standards for officiating a wedding, you may find that having a standard format for the wedding homily is helpful for service planning with the couple. Here are a few thoughts on preaching fruitful wedding sermons:

### You Aren't the Star

Do not draw unnecessary attention to yourself. Be warm and winsome, even funny, but don't turn the homily into a stand-up routine. Unfortunately, the standards of modern wedding ceremonies have so deteriorated that it seems couples are more interested in a zany voice than a pastoral one. Don't get on a soapbox about the state of marriage in the culture or anything else that would become a distraction. Lead the ceremony, but don't make yourself the center.

Christ is the star. The couple is the supporting cast. You're the director. Give your instructions and do your best to stay out of the way.

## Emphasize Covenant and Be Biblical

The point of officiating a wedding is administering covenant vows. This will involve some exposition and explanation of the marital covenant itself. Your wedding homily should help the bride and groom—and all their witnesses—soberly appraise the weight of a covenant commitment between two sinners before a holy God and sincerely celebrate how the Bible refers to the marital covenant as a picture of the gospel (Eph 5:32).

Eschew substantial meandering about romance and other sentimentalities and focus on what the Word of God says. Emphasize the grace behind the commitments the couple is making and the grace of God for sinners that rests behind the picture of marriage. This is also a prime opportunity for lost friends and family members of the bride and groom to hear the gospel, perhaps for the first time. Focus on the task at hand but bring the gospel to bear.

## Do Not Let the Couple Tell You What to Say

Don't let anyone write your homily for you. You can show it to them for review or input, but do not simply become the mouthpiece for whatever romantic message they may want dispensed. Insist that if they have chosen you to officiate, they are trusting you to speak appropriately and relevantly. One area you may want to watch closely in regard to this is in the vows exchanged by the couple. Show them sample vows reflecting a traditional expression. If they write their own vows, ask to help and encourage them to cover the same territory as the traditional vows do.

## Keep Your Message Short

A wedding is not a church service. It is not time to deliver a plenary talk on marriage. You are marrying a groom and bride. The important part is the gospel, the vows, and the celebratory witness of church, family, and friends. It is wise to keep your homily in the vicinity of fifteen minutes.

## Don't Administer Communion

Another fashionable entry in the modern wedding scene, especially among otherwise theologically minded couples, is the observance of the Lord's Supper. If you know this is the plan of the couple, dissuade it. Remind them that the supper is a family meal given to a local church and rightly observed in the gathering of a church body (1 Cor 11:27–34). Because a wedding is not a church service, the witnesses are not usually a gathered congregational body, and there are no pastoral authorities to whom the witnesses submit, it is not appropriate to co-opt the ordinance given *to the body*, even if it's to add a religious component to the ceremony.

# Preaching Funerals

An even greater privilege than officiating weddings, I'm convinced, is helping families grieve the loss of their loved ones. I have preached far more funerals than I have weddings, owing largely to the fact that I do not discriminate as narrowly as to which funerals I will preach. I can't think of a funeral request I've turned down, save for lack of availability.

As with weddings, you will have a prime opportunity to proclaim the good news of Jesus, only in this setting, the attention of the grieving is arrested and you will be able to spend more time on Jesus's death and subsequent victory over it. Death has startlingly interrupted mourners' business as usual, demanding their attention. Funeral attendees are more likely to be pondering spiritual subjects and willing to talk about the hope of salvation.

Of course, I have had people walk out of funerals I've preached over offense at my having talked (in their view) unnecessarily about sin and saving faith. In most of these cases, I am not just doing so due to my own conviction but also upon request of the mourning family or even occasionally upon request of the departed. I have walked with numerous saints to their finish line through all manner of suffering, and we have had lots of time to discuss what gospel emphases they would like me to proclaim at their funerals. Those are somber and sacred conversations.

Many pastors will find themselves the de facto chaplains of their communities, which means they will be requested to preach many funerals over the years, including many for unbelieving families of departed unbelievers. Here are some thoughts on shepherding in these moments and ministering well to unbelievers who have requested your funeral services:

## Presence Outshines Professionalism

When funeral home directors call to ask about availability to officiate a nonchurchgoing family's funeral for a loved one, the last thing I want to do is treat a death like business as usual. No family wants the pastor they've contacted to treat this aspect of his ministry as the florist does the flowers. Many times, they do not know what to ask for or what to expect. So after saying yes to the one making the funeral arrangements, I make contact with a member of the family to let them know I am thinking about them, praying for them, and would like to meet with a representative of the family at their earliest convenience to talk about the service.

Sometimes, families don't care to meet with me, and that's okay. But most often, I host a relative or two in my office, or I go to their homes to discuss the arrangements. But the first thing we always discuss is the departed. I may ask to see pictures. I recall one particular meeting around a family's kitchen table; my simple questions led to the family reminiscing together, telling funny stories about their son and brother. I helped start the discussion, but quickly became a mere observer. I didn't even say much in that meeting, but afterward they related to a church member how much my presence meant to them.

I have sat with the dying in hospitals, sharing the joy of Jesus with them in their final hours. I have counseled feuding family members in my office as they seek to honor their loved one while sorting through animosity long held with each other. I have held hands at a crime scene and at the morgue while a mother waited to identify her son's body. When a loved one dies, it is not business as usual for their family; it cannot be business as usual for the minister, either.

When possible, I also attend the postfuneral receptions and luncheons. I am introverted by nature, so it's sometimes difficult to strike up conversations with strangers. Thankfully, I'm not expected to be glad-handing and inserting myself into family conversations and sharing. But in my experience, simply being available has proven very helpful.

Never underestimate the power of presence. Coming alongside a family, even in silence—sometimes, especially in silence—beats making their needs look like something you're checking off your to-do list. Nevertheless, there *is* a sense in which professionalism can be expected, needed, and quite helpful.

## Professionalism Can Be Pastoral

I've learned from visiting with families deep in fresh grief that my taking on the burden of planning the funeral service without leaving much up to them can be very comforting. Few have put much forethought into these arrangements. And many families who are not churchgoing don't have much preconception about what a minister does, what a service ought to look like, or what's appropriate to include. I have been asked for permission about Scripture readings and reflections quite a bit; even many of the irreligious still maintain a respect for and deference to religious tradition and perceived religious authority. Families whose mourning takes precedence often defer to me in determining how a service goes.

When I go over a funeral service order with families, many times they simply nod and reply with some variation of "Whatever you think will be fine." I have learned that sometimes one of the best things I can do for these families is go into "professional mode." As they are handling family and friends coming into town, dealing with all the other goings-on attendant to the loss of a loved one, and just sorting through their own feelings, taking funeral service planning off their plate can be a major relief. The professionalism of good funeral home directors and morticians can be a calming service in this time, as well. Most families just don't know what's supposed to happen, so knowing that the minister does and will take care of it is a blessing.

## Proclamation Trumps Presumption

Here is the most sobering aspect of preaching a funeral for an (apparent) unbeliever. Funerals are rife with attempts at comforting assurance: "He's in a better place now." "She's up there dancing with Jesus." "He was a good kid, and now he's one of God's angels." If you decide to open up the floor for sharing from those gathered, the result can be a mishmash of pseudo-religious sentimentality, gritty stories about what a saintly cuss the old curmudgeon was, and sometimes borderline heresy.

When irreligious families who respect religion lose a loved one, they don't wrestle with whether the departed now faces eternal judgment. They assume their loved one will not. He or she was "a good person." My opinion on this custom—and better pastoral minds than mine may differ—is that it is the minister's job to relieve them of these assumptions *in a circumstantially appropriate way.*

No one has ever asked me, "Is my loved one in heaven?" because they all assume he or she is. In these moments, I remind myself that I am an invited guest to this family's mourning. It is better to speak my piece about the true gospel and rely on the Spirit to work the logic internally against mourners' assumptions than to directly and personally contradict people who are sorting out their grief and trying to offer comfort. There is a time for personal correction on these matters, but that time should probably not come in the middle of a funeral service.

At the same time, I cannot shake the reality that no one truly knows where anyone's eternal destiny lies the way God does. Salvation for the thief on the cross is enough precedent for us to remain humble on this point. I believe in deathbed conversions, not because grace is cheap but precisely because it's deep enough to cover a sinful person's long life of persistent disobedience. Declining to declare that the departed is in hell is not the same thing as denying the reality of hell.

## Proclamation Trusts Providence

Still, the minister's first loyalty is to Jesus Christ, not to any family. I customarily decline payment from unbelieving families for officiating their funerals because I never want to unwittingly bind my message to the dictates of those paying for it. When someone did not live a public life of faith, at the funeral I have never said anything about him or her being in heaven, playing a round of golf with God, or the like. It is just as important to avoid false assurance as it is to avoid presumptuous condemnations.

Instead, I typically outline briefly what the Bible says about grief, insist from the Scriptures that Jesus himself experienced grief, and then present the biblical story line of where death comes from, what it means for we who are still alive, and what it means for us in death. I make sure to say that those who reject Jesus will die eternally while those who repent of their sins and trust Jesus will live eternally, going to heaven when they die and enjoying the new heavens and the new earth on the future day of their own bodily resurrection.

By declining to presume where the departed has gone and committing to proclaim the eternal realities of any departed person in relation to Jesus, I am throwing myself onto the sovereignty of God, who will use his gospel to spiritually awaken his children to desire his Son. There are other opportunities for ministers who stay in touch with grieving families to more directly and personally share the gospel of Jesus later on. However, in the funeral service itself, a clear, concise, unequivocal proclamation of the good news, disconnected from presumptuous condemnation of or false assurance about the departed, is the wisest course.

## Reflections on the Ordinances

There is more in the worship service that preaches than the sermon itself. The liturgy (or worship order) tells a story that communicates implicitly and explicitly what is most important to a church. And the elements of that liturgy communicate, as well. The two ordinances instituted for the right exercise of church worship are baptism and communion, both of which are reflections of the gospel message.

Indeed, the celebration of baptism and the observation of communion in a worship gathering can be wonderful exclamation points adorning the explicit proclamation of God's word. Baptism and communion are both biblical applications of preaching, in fact, as they demonstrate, respectively, an unbeliever's saving response to having been changed by the proclamation of Christ's death and resurrection and a believer's faithful commitment to remembering the same.

As a prefatory note, I should mention that I am a committed Baptist and my views on the ordinances of baptism and communion (the Lord's Supper) reflect that commitment. Indeed, it is partly because of my understanding of what the Bible teaches about baptism and communion that I am a Baptist. If you do not share that commitment, I understand that some of what I write below may not comport with your own theological convictions, but perhaps you may learn something from my perspective, just as I likely have learned much from yours.

The two ordinances given to the church reflect two of the covenant markers given to the nation of Israel: circumcision and the Passover. Among a myriad of rituals and customs, these two became the visible markers of inclusion in God's covenant community. Thus there is, on one level, a continuity between baptism/communion and circumcision/Passover; but there is, on another level, a discontinuity. The spiritual freight is similar and the meanings of each correspond, but through the revelation of Jesus Christ, the recipients of these markers have changed. (I should note that even our brothers and sisters among the Reformed who insist on a strict continuity between circumcision and [infant] baptism acknowledge a discontinuity when they baptize their daughters.)

Here, then, are some thoughts on the ordinances relevant to the administration of them and to preaching generally:

## The Ordinances Do Not Merit Salvation, but They Are Bound Up with It

No work merits salvation but the work of Christ himself. Thus, while baptism and the Lord's Supper may rightly be seen as means of grace, neither *imparts* grace to us in their acts. The baptismal waters do not wash away sin. The bread and wine do not transfer meritorious grace to us. The ordinances are not salvific, but they are ways the church expresses *having received* salvation. In other words, despite the fact that nothing soteriologically meritorious is taking place in their practice, they are not empty rituals.

Baptism is, in effect, the biblical "sinner's prayer," the normative means by which one makes a profession of faith. The apostle Peter writes, "Baptism . . . now saves you, not as a removal of dirt from the body but as an appeal to God for a good conscience, through the resurrection of Jesus Christ" (1 Peter 3:21 ESV). Note that it is not the physical washing of baptism that imparts anything salvific, but the "appeal to God" which constitutes baptism. This is why I say baptism is the biblical sinner's prayer. This is also why "be baptized" so quickly follows the call to repent in the apostolic preaching.

Similarly, the Lord's Supper is a recurring profession of faith for the family of God. We proclaim Christ's death to each other and ourselves each time we partake of the meal (1 Cor 11:26).

## The Ordinances Are Symbols but Not *Mere* Symbols

There is nothing magical about the waters. There is nothing transubstantiated in the bread and wine. And yet we drain the ordinances of the grace that *is* there when we deem them *merely* symbols.

Protestants typically have no problem assigning spiritual weight to the ordinary preaching of the Word. God is empowering our words, using our speech to waken dead souls to his goodness. How could the ordinances not also constitute means of grace? "The bread that we break, is it not a participation in the body of Christ?" (1 Cor 10:16 ESV). "You were also circumcised in him with a circumcision not done with hands, by putting off the body of flesh, in the circumcision of Christ, when you were buried with him in baptism, in which you were also raised with him through faith in the working of God, who raised him from the dead" (Col 2:11–12 CSB). The ordinances are visible reminders of invisible grace. The practices strengthen our bodies, primarily through our obedience to observe them, which is integral to our sanctification. Additionally, through our public witness of them as an encouragement and participation in the body of Christ, they strengthen the church.

## Baptism Is an Entrance into the Covenant Community

As Paul puts it in 1 Corinthians 12:13, "For we were all baptized by one Spirit into one body—whether Jews or Greeks, whether slaves or free—and we were all given one Spirit to drink" (CSB).

In a previous section, I dissuaded the partaking of communion outside the gathering of a local body. Here, allow me to similarly dissuade the administering of baptism outside the same. Baptism is a symbol, not just of passing from death to life, but from alienation to reconcilia-tion—to God and to the church. Thus, individual believers disconnected from a church should not conduct baptisms, and those baptized should be seen as being baptized into the membership of a church.

Therefore, I offer two cautions for modern ministers. First, you should hesitate to baptize any person you would not immediately incorporate into full membership in your church. If you do not allow children of certain ages full membership privileges, you should not baptize them. (Conversely, if you do baptize them, confident in the credibility of their profession of faith, you should grant them mem-bership privileges, including participation at the Lord's Table, and treat them as full members of the church.)

Secondly, the practice of so-called "spontaneous baptisms" should be heavily scrutinized. From the case of the Ethiopian eunuch (Acts 8), we may say that exceptions might be made, and yet normally we should only baptize those who have given a credible profession of their faith—they can articulate the biblical gospel without coaching, they demonstrate a simple understanding of basic Christian ortho-doxy, they are able to testify to the work of the Spirit in their lives, they are conscious of their repentance and able to testify to it as well, and they can explain what baptism is and why they want to experi-ence it—and who will become discipled members of the church. In too many churches where spontaneous baptisms are practiced, the subjects are often left adrift to their own spiritual journey; churches do not disciple or sometimes even follow up with them.

## Baptism Pictures Christ's Work

We Baptists insist on immersion in the water as the required biblical practice, not simply based on the linguistic import of *baptizo*, but because the act portrays the death, burial, and resurrection of the Lord: "We were buried therefore with him by baptism into death, in order that, just as Christ was raised from the dead by the glory of the Father, we too might walk in newness of life" (Rom 6:4 ESV).

## Baptism Pictures Repentance

Baptism is a public profession of personal faith, the outward "acceptance" and proclamation of one's conversion to Christ. "John came," Mark writes, "baptizing in the wilderness and proclaiming a baptism of repentance for the forgiveness of sins" (Mark 1:4). "Repent and be baptized," Peter instructs the called at the end of his sermon (Acts 2:38). In fact, baptism is closely paired with repentance throughout the New Testament.

## The Lord's Supper Is a Memorial Meal

"Do this in remembrance of me" (Luke 22:19). We take of the bread to remind us of Christ's flesh submitted in our place. We take of the cup to remind us of Christ's blood shed to propitiate God's wrath on our behalf. We take the meal because it is a picture of the very work of grace in Christ's cross. It is how we echo Paul's "reminder" (1 Cor 15:1) of the gospel. It is how we remind ourselves and each other of Jesus's sacrifice.

## The Lord's Supper Is a Covenant Meal

"This cup is the new covenant in my blood, which is poured out for you" (Luke 22:20). The very bread and wine representing the provision of Christ are a picture of God's faithfulness to his people. We sin, and yet he maintains the covenant. We fail, yet he never forsakes. We forget, and yet he always remembers. The meal is a reminder that Christ's sacrifice was the ultimate provision from the covenant-keeping God.

## The Lord's Supper Is a Worship Meal

"For whenever you eat this bread and drink this cup, you proclaim the Lord's death until he comes" (1 Cor 11:26). Communion is a kind of preaching of the gospel. And eating is a kind of worship in response to it. We take the meal in the worship gathering because it constitutes one of the signs of a rightly ordered church but also because it is an act of submissive service to the Lord. We pledge that our subsistence is found in God alone through this meal. That is a declaration of worship. We pledge allegiance to God in the meal. That is an ascription of worship.

## The Lord's Supper Is a Family Meal

"So then, my brothers and sisters, when you gather to eat, you should all eat together" (1 Cor 11:33). This is one reason why I do not encourage the taking of communion outside the worship service. Weddings, small groups, conferences, and other meetings of a subset of the church (men's or women's retreat, youth group, etc.) are not gatherings of the body, but parts of the body. The Lord's Supper is a corporate meal. It is meant for the body and is to be taken together by the body, not individual body parts. The only exception to this general rule I would make is in the case of those permanently hindered from attending worship—shut-ins and those in nursing homes, etc.

Within the ordinary practice of corporate communion, I also think the wise pastor will "fence the table," making it clear to those gathered that the meal is only for those who are baptized believers in the Lord Jesus (1 Cor 11:27–29).

This is admittedly not a full treatment of the ordinances, but some general thoughts related to our consideration and administration of them. As the conducting of baptism and communion are aspects of the pastoral office and related to the preaching of the gospel, I include them here, hoping they will encourage you. For your further consideration, especially with the newer ministers in mind, I encourage you to work through the following questions carefully:

1. How do you know someone is ready to be baptized?
2. If someone has been baptized as an infant in a gospel-affirming Presbyterian church or other Protestant Reformed

tradition, should they be admitted to membership in a Baptist church? Why or why not?

3. If someone came to you with a story of early baptism (as a believer) but now doubts the legitimacy of their baptism and seeks to be baptized again, how would you counsel them?

4. What is the relationship between baptism and the Lord's Supper?

5. How often should local churches observe the Lord's Supper? Why?

6. Does it matter what kind of elements we use in the Lord's Supper? Can we use tortilla chips and grape soda? Why or why not?

7. Does it matter if we drink from a cup, or can we practice intinction (dipping the bread in the cup)?

8. What are the benefits/drawbacks of taking communion at "stations" or from servants versus passing the elements throughout the congregation?

9. Should pastors fence the table in any way and, if so, how? Should you practice closed communion (only members of your church)? Close communion (only members of any gospel-believing church)? Open communion (anyone)?

In all of these practicalities related to preaching, we continue to see how preaching exists not primarily as a performative function of the church, but as a pastoral one. Elders are designated for "prayer and the ministry of the word" (Acts 2:4), but we see how they may be involved in the work of "serving tables," as communion is both a work of proclamation and an act of pastoral care. It is to that pastoral care that we will turn in the next chapter.

## For Reflection

1. What component of sermon preparation do you struggle with most? Why?

2. What is your plan for developing strength in that area of weakness?

3. What is your position on wedding ceremonies? Are there any you would not officiate? Explain.

4. How would you explain the Lord's Supper to an unbeliever?

5. What are some ways to communicate the gospel in a sermon that do not feel like an artificial "tack-on" at the end of your message?

## For Further Study:

Lloyd-Jones, D. Martyn. *Preaching and Preachers*. 40th anniversary ed. Grand Rapids: Zondervan, 2012.

No study of gospel-centered preaching would be complete without wading into this classic work from perhaps the greatest Reformed preacher of the twentieth century. I recommend the 40th anniversary edition of the text, which also includes reflective essays from contemporary preachers like Mark Dever, Tim Keller, and John Piper.

Motyer, Alec. *Preaching? Simple Teaching on Simply Preaching*. Fearn, Scotland: Christian Focus Publications, 2013.

This book from a renowned biblical scholar provides a wonderful overview of the preacher's biblical aims and motivations with a focus on order and organization.

Robinson, Haddon W. *Biblical Preaching: The Development and Delivery of Expository Messages*. 3rd ed. Grand Rapids: Baker, 2014.

Still the go-to textbook in countless preaching classes in seminaries today, *Biblical Preaching* is especially helpful in instructing on the translation of an exegetical outline into a homiletical outline, an art form mastered by still too few preachers today.

# CHAPTER 6

# CARING

From my ministry vantage point helping train men for the pastorate and traveling and meeting young and aspiring pastors around the world, I have been greatly encouraged by what I can only call the *pastoral temperament* I sense among the younger generation. What I mean is, I sense—and I hope that I'm right—that something that has come alongside the gospel recovery movement is not just a recovery of theology, expositional preaching, missional church planting, and the like but also a recovery of the active and intentional shepherding of the people of God. Our ancestors used to call this intentional shepherding "the curing of souls."

A lot of us still remember the *winning* of souls, and we employ that concept in a variety of ways, from end-of-service invitations to door-to-door evangelism or gospel sharing in backyards and coffee shops and airplane seats. But the curing of souls has fallen on hard times. You get the impression from some church promotional material that our only job is to win the soul, and then the soul is really sort of on its own. But Jesus did not say simply to go out into the world and make *converts* of all peoples; he said to make *disciples*. And this means the pastoral enterprise cannot begin and end with public proclamation and private planning—it must be applied in personal care.

The phrase is antiquated today, of course—curing souls may conjure up the image of an old-timey physician or apothecary, promising some magical elixir for our spiritual maladies. Or, more crudely, it may simply remind others of curing meat! But while the wording may be old-fashioned, I certainly hope the concept is not.

To those in the church committed not just to preaching and teaching and prayer—the primary tasks of the church elder, to be sure—but also to home and hospital visitation, counseling, personal discipleship—to helping people think, helping people obey, and helping people die—I want to offer my warmest thanks and profoundest salute. And to those who seem to be falling behind in this vital area, I hope what follows will serve as a gracious exhortation to repentance.

And to those just starting out, let this chapter serve as a reminder that the work of pastoring is sheep work—tending, feeding, nurturing. Preaching may be the most important thing a pastor does, but if he does not do the relational work of pastoral care, he will find fewer and fewer listening in the end.

## The Nature of Pastoral Care

In 1 Thessalonians 2:7–8, the apostle Paul writes:

> But we were gentle among you, like a nursing mother taking care of her own children. So, being affectionately desirous of you, we were ready to share with you not only the gospel of God but also our own selves, because you had become very dear to us. (ESV)

The nursing mother, of course, is not the dominant model of the pastoral vocation marketed today. I have never seen a ministry conference advertised as "The Pastor as Nursing Mother." But this is exactly the image that Paul is here introducing as emblematic of the pastoral task. Why does he use this maternal image to reflect "being affectionately desirous" of his flock and sharing not only the gospel but his very self with them? I think Paul uses the image to illustrate what pastoral care is like in at least three ways:

## Pastoral Care Is the Overflow of Love

I didn't nurse my children, of course, but I do remember getting up with them in the middle of the night and preparing a bottle and feeding and rocking them. As fussy and inconsolable as babies can sometimes be, I don't know if I've ever felt more connected to my daughters than when cradling them up close, feeding them, singing to them, rocking them, and soothing them. I often started that routine exasperated and frustrated, but I almost never ended it that way.

Peter says to "shepherd the flock of God that is among you" (1 Peter 5:2 ESV), something you cannot do if you're not actually *among* the flock. Something spiritual happens when we get up close, share meals with our people, weep with them, remind them gently of the gospel, listen to their stories, and hold their hands when they're hurting or dying. You cannot experience this if you see the people of your church as projects rather than people. You cannot experience this if your ministry is driven largely out of ambition or aspiration. It must be driven by love.

Paul calls this love "affectionate desire." When Jesus looks out on the crowd and says that they are harassed and helpless like sheep without a shepherd, he is broken inside over them (Matt 9:36; Mark 6:34). If you struggle to feel this way about your church, ask yourself why. Ask God to help you. And then put yourself in positions to have your heart shaped more toward them. This is why Paul describes his presence as "gentle" and why one of the biblical qualifications for eldership is gentleness (1 Tim 3:3). It's also one of the fruits of the Spirit (Gal 5:22–23). So, if you're not a gentle person, not only are you disqualifying yourself from ministry, you have reason to test your salvation to see if you are in the faith.

## Pastoral Care Is an Act of Nurture

The nursing mom is feeding her child. She isn't neglectful. She isn't outsourcing the work. Remember that Jesus didn't say to Peter, "Teach the sheep to self-feed." He said, "Feed my lambs" (John 21:15). Pastor, do not look at your church primarily as a recruiting station, an event center, or a spiritual production but as a pasture where the sheep are nourished.

And you must take care regarding what you feed your sheep. If you want them to be nourished, built up in their faith, and empowered to follow Christ day by day, you must feed them grace. The finished work of Christ announced in the gospel is the only power prescribed in the Scriptures for growth in godliness. You can't inject anything into the law that will make it do what the simple, pure feast of the gospel will. Make sure you provide enough opportunities to feed on the gospel, so that they never lack the sustenance they need to live and grow.

## Pastoral Care Is an Act of Self-Giving

The nursing mom brings her baby to her breast. She is giving of herself. She cannot give what she doesn't have. This is why Paul connects the image to "sharing our very selves" with the church at Thessalonica.

Pastoral care is costly. It doesn't just hurt our brains; it can hurt our hearts. Sometimes sheep bite. The weight of ministry will keep us up at night. Sometimes it will make us feel drained. In 2 Corinthians 11, Paul talks about the anxiety he feels for all the churches. Godly pastors know what he means by this—the spiritual weight of *responsibility* (2 Cor 11:28). If your ministry is comfortable, you may not actually be doing ministry. Godly pastoral care means taking the uncomfortable risk of self-giving.

This means, pastors, that to give adequate care, we must give adequate time to be nourished ourselves. We cannot give what we don't have. This is not a call to be self-centered but to be self-aware. (I will say more about this in subsequent chapters.)

During my last pastorate, one dear lady who began as one of my most serious scrutinizers became one of my biggest supporters. When you can turn a critic into a colleague, something extraordinary has happened because usually it runs the other way! But this woman watched me for several years up close and asked me lots of questions about my motives and intentions. She saw me at my best and at my worst. She got a piece of my heart. Eventually, she ended up being the last saint I had the privilege of helping pass into glory; hers was the last funeral I preached before my time of service there ended. Over several months as she was dying, I was one of the few she permitted to enter her hospice room at will—to talk, to pray, or to read Scripture with her. Why? Because when I first came, I was just "the preacher." But I had become, over time, her *pastor*.

This isn't new or innovative. And it's not rocket science. But it is vital to the work of the minister and to the life of his congregation. Godly pastoral care is the overflow of nurturing, self-giving love.

The nature of pastoral care, then—what care is and what it's made of—manifests itself in a heart toward others. The pastoral nature results in a pastoral posture, the "visible heart" of shepherding.

## The Heart of Pastoral Care

Consider the disposition of Paul in his pastoral prayer over the church at Philippi:

> I thank my God in all my remembrance of you, always in every prayer of mine for you all making my prayer with joy, because of your partnership in the gospel from the first day until now. And I am sure of this, that he who began a good work in you will bring

it to completion at the day of Jesus Christ. It is right for me to feel this way about you all, because I hold you in my heart, for you are all partakers with me of grace, both in my imprisonment and in the defense and confirmation of the gospel. For God is my witness, how I yearn for you all with the affection of Christ Jesus. And it is my prayer that your love may abound more and more, with knowledge and all discernment, so that you may approve what is excellent, and so be pure and blameless for the day of Christ, filled with the fruit of righteousness that comes through Jesus Christ, to the glory and praise of God. (Phil 1:3–11 ESV)

Paul is writing this letter while under house arrest in Rome, likely about fourteen years or so after he'd planted this church. This is one of his most personal letters, and this intimacy is probably because of the depth of his own investment in it. The church at Philippi is the first church planted in Europe, and the circumstances around it are described in Acts. The second missionary journey begins with a falling-out between Paul and Barnabas over the inclusion of Mark (Acts 15:36–41). The bitterness of that experience remains as Paul and Silas set out. It's on this missionary journey that Paul meets Timothy, beginning a relationship that would bring him great joy (Acts 16:1–3). And it's on this journey that he had the vision of Macedonians crying out, "Come and help us" (Acts 16:9), so he goes straight there and ends up in Philippi. Paul and Silas's preaching makes more than a few converts, including Lydia, a demoniac slave girl, and the Philippian jailer.

The point of these observations is to show that Paul's blood, sweat, and tears are in this church. While he isn't there personally to shepherd it as a local elder, he not only has authority over it as its apostolic founder, he feels a deep, personal kinship with it. His heart is melded to this church, which is, in the nonidolatrous sense, the aim of every pastoral heart. From this heartfelt, prayerful exultation, we learn a reliable pattern for doing church ministry; his letter describes a posture appropriate for anybody invested in their church, but especially for leaders and pastors. How is that pastoral posture embodied?

## A Heart That Is for the Church

Fundamentally, the pastor's posture ought to be driven by a heart *for* his church; that is, a heart that is *for* his people, not against them.

A posture that is against the church may be expressed in different ways. There's the *heart of discontent* with our church, where we carry around a well-nursed self-pity, a sense of not being appreciated or understood or respected. There's the *victim's heart*, where we constantly see our church as a burden, an impediment, or even an enemy, but more often as "our cross to bear." We can carry a *heart of disappointment* or even anger toward our church for not being zealous enough about the gospel, for not being active enough in missionary efforts, or for being too much of one thing and not enough of another. Others have a *controlling heart*, by which we either dominate our church like a little religious dictator or, more often, by which we see the church as a big project, an experiment in which we can work out our theories, strategy, leadership, and entrepreneurship. There's a *heart of wish-fulfillment*, in which we project our hopes, dreams, and insecurities onto the church in the hopes that it will fulfill or validate our intellect, gifts, or reason for existence. There's the *distant heart*—cold and aloof, withdrawn and insular.

The problem with all of these alternative heart postures (and more I didn't mention) is that they fundamentally set us up to be against our churches. They are postures of *us versus them*. And once you start harboring in your heart rehearsed thoughts of us versus them, you cease being your church's advocate and begin siding with her Accuser.

There's a way to intercede that's basically an echo of the Accuser: "Lord, look at these awful people you've given me—think of how much I could get done if not for them!" Sometimes you pray prayers like that, and it's okay insofar as you're just being real with God. But our habit should be to intercede in a way that basically echoes Christ our Advocate: "Oh Lord, I don't know what you're doing with these people, but I care about them, I love them, and I know you're working everything toward the good of those who love you. What a privilege it is to speak for you to them and to shepherd them under you! Please make us all look more like Jesus."

We get a glimpse into Paul's heart as he intercedes for the people in Philippians 1:3–6. I notice three heart postures in those 3 verses: gratitude (v. 3), joy (v. 4), confidence/hope (v. 6). These postures characterize his prayer for the Philippians and position him not as his church's accuser but as her advocate. He's in the place of intercession, which is a place of advocacy. Not in the grumbling sense but in the *joyful, thankful, confident sense*. Paul didn't see the church at Philippi as a project, but as a partnership. He didn't see them as liabilities, but as lambs. He knew lambs require tending, and his prayers reflect that nurturing posture.

Moses reflects the same posture when he intercedes for the Israelites. In Exodus 32, after the golden calf fiasco, he's angry and frustrated, but he essentially says to the Lord, "Forgive them. But if you can't, blot *me* out of the book of life. Take me instead." Paul is willing to make the same personal sacrifice in Romans 9:3: "For I could wish that I myself were cursed and cut off from Christ for the benefit of my brothers and sisters, my own flesh and blood" (CSB). You actually have to love people if you're going to say stuff like that to God.

No one had a more important ministry than Jesus. And yet you notice, time and time again, how patient he was with interruptions, diversions, and pastoral excursions. Why? Because his fundamental posture toward people who were in need of shepherding was not irritation or frustration but a broken-in-the-guts kind of compassion.

I recall visiting one of our ladies in the hospital after a knee surgery. You should have seen her look of surprise when she saw me at her door to come to her bedside!

"I can't believe you'd come see me," she said.

"Why?" I asked.

"Because you're so busy."

"Sister," I said, "this is what I'm busy doing!"

She was not an interruption in my ministry week. She *was* the ministry.

The heart of ministry is a heart that doesn't see people as the interruption to your ministry, but sees the interruptions *as* the ministry. The posture of pastoral care is inclined toward the church. But it isn't simply moving toward. It is willing to receive and to be vulnerable.

## A Heart That Is Open to the Church

Having a heart for the church is more about the minister's *private* disposition, how he carries the church internally, what he thinks about when he thinks about the church. Having a heart that is open to the church is about our *public* disposition. It involves what the pastor actually says and does. When people see that you love them, they will be more inclined to trust you. As it's been said, "If they know you love them, you can say anything to them."

Now, it's entirely possible to love the church while you're in your study or lying awake in bed at night. In fact, nearly all ministers do that, I'm sure. Their sermon prep, bedtime prayers, daily quiet and lonely times are spent in prayerful love for the church. But a love unexpressed is not a love fully embraced. We need a heart for the church that's vulnerable before the church. This involves, at the very least, proximity. But on top of that, it involves a kind of transparency, honesty, and authenticity.

Notice how close Paul gets in Philippians 1:7–8; he's evincing a holy transparency. He's telling them how he feels about them. He notes what they share (suffering), how they partner, and their mutual affection. In 2 Corinthians 6:11–13, Paul writes to a different church: "We have spoken freely to you, Corinthians; our heart is wide open. You are not restricted by us, but you are restricted in your own affections. In return (I speak as to children) widen your hearts also" (ESV). His heart is "wide open" to the Corinthians. I don't know if you know anything about the church at Corinth at this time, but I guarantee you that your church is healthier.

What does an open heart look like? It probably doesn't wear its feelings on its sleeve, but is certainly transparent in its dispositions. An open-hearted pastor has developed a thick skin but remains tender. An open heart feels no compulsion to self-protect or put on airs. An open heart sees no advantage in putting up a facade. An open heart knows it is hidden with Christ in God, so there is nothing left to hide. An open heart bleeds out grace. An open heart is generous with its affections. An open heart is hospitable to the joys and pains of others. It rejoices with those who rejoice and weeps with those who weep. An open heart sits across the table from another open heart and does not check its watch. An open heart feels the circumstances in which it finds itself but, inhabited by the Holy Spirit, is tuned to the deeper frequency of the gospel's indomitable joy. A heart wide open speaks freely and love comes out.

At the end of every worship service at my last church, after we'd corporately prayed a blessing over our community and sung the "Doxology," I used to dismiss my congregation with these words: "I love you." Why? Well, because I loved my church! I looked at them and I couldn't help saying it. But I made it a discipline to say "I love you" so they'd know it's okay to say such things to people who aren't children or spouses; so they'd know that their pastor—who might have just been challenging them or even rebuking them in the midst of proclaiming the gospel to them—is doing so out of love; and so they will have a reference point for the freedom I feel to cry, laugh, walk around, yell, whisper, and any other sorts of things that may be involved in exulting in the Scriptures.

Over time, I began to hear the call back "We love you too" from more and more corners. They were widening their hearts also.

I shared this once on a panel at a conference and another pastor kind of made fun of it. Not really, but just playfully. He said, "I can't imagine saying that to my church . . ." I laughed at that but replied, "You know, it occurred to me that there are people who file into that building every Sunday morning who probably haven't heard anyone say 'I love you' in days, weeks, maybe even years. And here's someone who is a representative for God, telling them in a heartfelt way, 'I love you.' Don't underestimate the impact of that."

The problem is not saying it, but saying it without demonstrating it. A heart that's open isn't just generous with loving words but also loving service. In other words, they won't believe it if they don't feel it. If your preaching is characterized by a tone of legality or condemnation, or your demeanor is consistently stern or firm, "I love you" is a dare to doubt. And if you only preach it but never put it into action, you similarly tempt them to disbelief. In an introduction to Richard Baxter's *Dying Thoughts*, Edward Donnelly writes, "In order to be a true preacher a man must be a true pastor."[1]

I once had to kick a heretic out of my church. He had come quietly enough, blending in with the sheep, but I noticed his quarrelsomeness over time. His doctrine was dangerous. He denied the Trinity. He insisted on works righteousness. I hoped he'd hear our message and be cut to the quick, but he was preoccupied with his own message. The trouble was that he wanted my flock to be as preoccupied with it as he was. I took him aside and said, "Look, you are more than welcome to attend worship here, but I cannot have you trying to teach my people. We don't believe what you believe, and I have a responsibility to protect them from false teaching. If you want to attend, please do so without cornering people and trying

---

1. Edward Donnelly, introduction to *Dying Thoughts*, by Richard Baxter (Carlisle, PA: Banner of Truth, 2009), xvii.

to proselytize them." He agreed but kept doing it. I warned him a second time (Titus 3:10–11). He assured me he would finally quit.

One Sunday when I was done preaching, the service had just ended, and I hadn't even descended from the pulpit, this fellow made a beeline to the edge of the stage and began to debate a point in my sermon. I was tired but tried to explain. He pressed more intently. He was trying to foist legalism upon me. I told him I'd already warned him twice not to do that in the church. He looked me in the eyes and said, "Always learning, never coming to the truth."

Something in me broke. I rose up and raised my voice. Pointing to him and then to the door, I said, "Get your things and get out and don't come back." His eyes got wide and he sheepishly exited the church. He did not return, though I later learned he was making a tour of other churches in the area and basically experiencing the same thing each time.

I am confident that what I felt in the moment of kicking this fellow out of the church was not a need to be right or a need to win a theological argument. What I felt was an instinctive, even mother-bear kind of protectiveness over the sheep of my flock, whom I had suddenly sensed were in danger. I was being a shepherd.

Later, I followed up with the church to explain because I was afraid some folks would think I was mean or rude or condemnatory. The response I received from one dear lady actually typified the response I received generally: "Jared, we know that you did that because you felt you needed to, and while I don't know the whole story about it, I trust that you were doing something in the best interest of the church."

Why did she think that? Probably because I didn't have a habit of yelling at anybody, or even being stern with people. If I appeared to become righteously indignant in that moment, they could reason that perhaps the situation actually called for it. I was not prone to flying off the handle at every criticism or challenge. But, because this lamb believed I loved her, she trusted that my actions were an expression of that.

When you open your heart to your people, what you discover over time is that you want better things for them and for the church than the metrics promoted by pragmatists. You do not see your people as warm bodies or "giving units" but as precious souls. As such, your pastoral posture is inclined toward what matters most.

## A Heart That Values Sanctification over Success

The problem with a growing church isn't primarily logistical. It's spiritual.

Sure, there are issues of increasing complexity as a church grows numerically—things related to budgetary needs, facility impact, seating capacity, parking spaces, scaling administration accordingly, etc. Those are important and necessary things you have to deal with. As we like to say, those are "good problems to have."

But a heart for the church and open to the church isn't simply thinking about the logistical problems of growth but also the spiritual problems of growth. Who's going to shepherd all these sheep? How are they going to be cared for? Who is going to disciple them? Who is going to walk alongside them, inquire as to their spiritual state, and nurture them to maturity?

And then, more generally, the more people you have, the more sinners you have in close proximity; just a few sinners are already hard to deal with, especially given that it is sinners who are trying to deal with them! As people gather, they bring their sins with them. But they also bring their anxieties, their wounds, their trauma, their "baggage," their misunderstandings, their doubts, and their ignorance. They bring their sense of loneliness, their sense of abandonment, and their sense of feeling left out, left behind, or left outside. They bring their suffering and their grief. When your doors open on Sunday morning, a world of brokenness files in.

Who feels qualified for such a weighty reality as this? The

Spirit-filled pastor says, "I am in way over my head." It's the fleshly pastor who says, "I know *exactly* how to manage this."

Seen facing this challenge in Philippians 1, Paul goes to God, the only power strong enough to accomplish what God means for the church to accomplish. The whole passage has the mark of prayer, especially given verses 3–4: "I thank my God in all my remembrance of you, always in every prayer of mine . . ." What does he pray *for* in verse 9? Not their numbers, but their love—their love in knowledge and discernment. What does he pray is filled? Not their gatherings with bodies, but their souls with the fruit of righteousness. Is it wrong to pray for numbers and full gatherings? Absolutely not. You'd be abnormal if you didn't pray for such things. But there are things "superior," Paul says, to outward growth.

You even see this in the way Paul takes pride in the churches. It's not their success that he takes pride in but they themselves:

> [O]n the day of our Lord Jesus you will boast of us as we will boast of you.
>
> —2 CORINTHIANS 1:14 ESV

> So give proof before the churches of your love and of our boasting about you to these men.
>
> —2 CORINTHIANS 8:24 ESV

> I boast about you to the people of Macedonia.
>
> —2 CORINTHIANS 9:2 ESV

> For what is our hope or joy or crown of boasting before our Lord Jesus at his coming? Is it not you?
>
> —1 THESSALONIANS 2:19 ESV

Are you wrong to care about full sanctuaries? No. But please note that Paul never writes to any of the churches, "How many are you running?" His heart treasures spiritual growth over numeric growth. They aren't always mutually exclusive, but neither are they synonymous.

I hope you get your God-shaped heart's desire when it comes to your dream for your church and that you'll be bursting at the seams with people and with glory! But what if God only grants you the glory? What if his plan for your church is not success but sanctification? What if his plan for you—your ministry, your heart—is not success but drawing you so near to him in your dependence, your disappointment, and your devastation that you become more like Christ? Would that be, in the end, delicious to you?

The truth is that the Lord may not be committed to *our* success. But here's the promise in this: he *is* committed to *his*. And because of that, he is committed to us becoming more like his Son. He will make sure we are delivered before his presence at the last day, blameless with great joy (Jude 24). He is committed to completing the work he began in us (Phil 1:6).

We cannot be Jesus to your people. Jesus is more than enough. But we can represent the heart of Jesus to them. And the closer we get to Christ's heart of compassion ourselves, the better—the more supernaturally and the more instinctively—we will be able to do that for them.

Christ's heart is for you, pastor. His heart is open to you. And you can take heart in your smallness or suffering, because his heart is committed to your sanctification. His posture toward you can become, by his grace, your posture toward them.

## The Practice of Pastoral Care

Thus far, we've seen that the posture of pastoral care is an open-hearted advocacy for the church. This means, undoubtedly, a regular *drawing near*. The shepherd's blood, sweat, and tears are spent in the tending and feeding of the sheep. Just as the Son descended and dwelt among us (John 1:14), the pastor mingles with the flock, living as one with them and yet leading the way in developing a culture of grace and truth. The purpose of pastoral care, as in preaching, is to point people to Jesus. Point away from yourself to the fountain of grace in Christ. He is our Physician and Good Shepherd. He is the one who always lives to intercede for us (Heb 7:25).

Pastoral care can go awry not only when it is neglected but also when it is self-referential, as when a pastor cultivates a kind of co-dependency with his flock. He becomes their functional messiah. He is not pointing to Jesus; he is indulging his need to be needed. And many congregations are perfectly happy with this arrangement. They exist to express the need for ministry, and their pastor lives to supply it. This is a recipe for disaster. It is congregational idolatry.

But neglect is a real danger, as well. Especially as a church grows and its needs increase, if there has not been an appropriate scaling of elder plurality or other systems by which the body can care for itself—conforming closely to the New Testament "one another"s—the end result is very often a church that is successfully preached at but not healthfully cared for.

This is a special danger for the introverted or otherwise independently minded minister. The temptation is to hole up in one's study all week, studying, writing, and praying. That is vital work, indispensable to the office of the pastorate. But if you get to the end of your week and you don't have at least a little wool on your jacket, you may not be a shepherd.

Extroverted pastors, on the other hand, may embrace the illusion of real pastoral care and closeness with the flock because of their constant interaction with members of the church. The temptation for the extrovert, often more subtle than that facing introverts, is to mistake superficial conversations and feeding off the energy of interaction with actual self-sacrificial care and empathy. Some of the pastors I've observed to have the lowest "emotional intelligence" have been high-functioning extroverts unclear on the distinction between enjoying being with people and establishing meaningful relationships.

Draw near. Put others' needs before your own. And, above all, point people to Jesus for their satisfaction, comfort, and joy. The following provides a few words of counsel for those engaged in the precious practice of pastoral care in various contexts:

## Shut-Ins and Nursing Homes

It may be fair to say that the true measure of a pastor is how willing he is to spend time with people who can do nothing for him. There are members of our flocks who cannot even fill a seat. They cannot contribute to the budget, except perhaps meagerly. They do not wield any significant influence among the congregation. They can't even "talk us up" in town. Spending time with them is *for them*. It will cost us time we can't get back. It will not show any immediate returns on leadership investments. And for all these reasons, visiting shut-ins and folks in nursing homes is some of the most Christlike work you can do.

In my last pastorate, there were a number of older widows who struggled to attend church. I made it a habit to visit them about once a month, sometimes more frequently in "slower" ministry seasons. I had to force myself to put these appointments in the calendar. In my context, it involved significant driving in rural areas. "Making the rounds" could take half a day or even an entire day. To my shame, I dragged my feet to carry out this ministry. But I never, ever regretted it. I always walked out of these visits feeling the love of God in a more profound way than I had going in.

It is true that these folks cannot often do anything for us in terms of church growth or PR in the congregation. But neither do they often put inordinate expectations or burdens on us. They are usually just glad for the visit, eager to talk about their families or their childhoods. They are usually very hungry to be heard. And here you are, showing them in a real way the love of Jesus, who is always there to listen.

If you are reluctant to do this work, repent and reengage. You won't regret it.

## Hospitals

Do not underestimate the power of even a short check-in with any of your members in the hospital, especially older members. Bring concern and cheer, depending on the nature of the stay, of course. It is usually best to keep visits short—not so short as to appear as though you are simply "popping in" but not so long as to risk making the patient uncomfortable.

Depending on what someone was in the hospital for, I usually visited for about an hour. If someone is in an emergency situation, I may stay longer. I've sat in waiting rooms with families for long hours through the night as the situation with their loved one looked disconcerting. For those recovering from routine or nonthreatening surgery and for those who've given birth, an hour is usually the longest I would visit.

Younger patients tend to be least comfortable with visits in these situations, and older patients tend to be more open to them; but know your sheep well, and ask them or family members about the appropriateness of a visit if you're unsure. As a general rule, the more intimate and personal the nature of the illness or surgery, the more modesty you should adopt and the more intentional you should be in inquiring ahead of time. For example, a tonsillectomy or broken arm will require less discretion on your part than a mastectomy, miscarriage, or hernia repair.

On your visit, be conversational. Ask questions and listen. Definitely pray for the patient. And do not underestimate appropriate touch. A hand on the shoulder of a man or holding the hand of an older woman in these situations, especially during prayer, can be extremely helpful to them spiritually.

## Home Visits

This practice is becoming rarer and rarer today. Younger people tend not to like home visits from pastors and tend to prefer appointments in places like coffee shops or cafes. Christians in older generations tend to be more open. In some contexts, the "pop-in" home visit is still appreciated and even expected. In an increasing number of others, it is seen as intrusive and unwelcome. Knowing your flock is critical in this regard.

Pastoral home visits can still be greatly beneficial to the life of the body, however, and ministers should consider them a valid alternative with many members to meeting in the pastor's office. Especially if conversation is expected to become serious or if counseling may be involved, a visit in the pastor's office can feel too formal and uncomfortable, like going to the principal's office. Many members will be more comfortable on their "home turf" than in yours. And they may appreciate your willingness to enter into their world and into their schedule rather than always expecting members to work around yours. Another benefit to an "away" visit is that you can end the meeting on time by indicating your need to leave. This is much easier than expressing to a visiting member that it is time for them to leave your office.

Exercise wisdom about the various circumstances that home visits may entail: Will there be appropriate safety and accountability for all parties? Should you bring another elder along as a witness and additional caregiver? Should you invite your wife to come in order to add a female perspective? Making sure that the situation feels safe to all parties and observers is both prudent and loving.

## Office Visits

If meeting with someone in your office, do whatever you can to be hospitable and ensure their comfort. Don't sit behind your desk if you can help it. Don't appear distracted or preoccupied with other office matters while you're meeting, lest you give the impression that your guest is an intrusion or interruption.

## Workplace Visits

Depending on the nature of the employment of your church members, consider visiting them at their places of work or business. In my last context, I had a number of men who worked blue collar jobs, mostly outdoors, and it was actually fun taking time to see their daily routines in action. Men especially appreciate this kind of visitation. It makes them feel honored and cared for. They appreciate your interest in their daily life, your willingness to see what life is like outside the church.

## Visiting Women

It is not advisable to meet with women alone.[2] I know that in this current cultural moment, the so-called "Billy Graham Rule" is not much in fashion. Women have felt dishonored by this practice, and certainly there is a way to communicate this standard that does dishonor women. We never want to suggest that we adhere to this practice because we view all women as potential temptresses or because we ourselves lack self-control. Nevertheless, it is still a good standard for most pastoral contexts. For one thing, it shows appropriate care for women by demonstrating that we are interested in their comfort and safety. And it also will show great honor to her husband (present or future) and your wife.

The presumption is not that every one-on-one meeting between a pastor and a female congregant is always a pretext for immorality or abuse; this general rule is a safeguard against accusations (typically from the outside) and a provision of care. A male pastor meeting with a lone woman, for whatever reason, constitutes a significant power differential. Having another woman present,

---

2. Indeed, it may not be advisable to meet with any person alone if they are a member of a more vulnerable demographic—women, teens or young adults, whether male or female, etc. Given the growing rate of public cases of abuse and other mistreatment, pastors should exercise great care in our meetings with members of vulnerable populations—not because every meeting is potentially tempting to us or the one we're meeting with but because creating a safe and secure environment for all involved should be our top priority.

whether your wife or a friend of the woman's or an older lady from church, can be a way to communicate that you are interested in your member's comfort and support.

I do not think it is necessary to be dogmatic about this, and pastoral instincts (and contexts) may differ in such a way that you find this rule dispensable; but it is still a helpful standard for many pastors.

## Principles for Pastoral Counseling

Pastors regularly available to their congregations will undoubtedly receive regular requests for counseling. Helping people apply biblical wisdom and encouraging them in their followship of Jesus in the midst of their grief, doubt, fear, or confusion is vital work for faithful shepherds.

Pastoral counseling should first and foremost be seen as a vital aspect of a pastor's discipleship. Remember that you are pointing people to Jesus. He is their Rock. He is their comfort. He is their joy and satisfaction.

People are extremely complex creatures. We are made in the image of God and yet are profoundly broken. Our sin taints everything. Our woundedness impacts everything. Helping church members distinguish between appropriate and inappropriate feelings and fears is both spiritually and time intensive.

Justice to the scope of concerns related to pastoral counseling cannot be done in one section in one chapter of a book, but here I offer some reflections from my experience with this part of pastoral care.

### Ask Questions and Listen a Lot

The second worst counselors don't say much. The worst counselors never shut up. Ask lots of questions and spend a lot of time listening. This is how you show your member you care about them, that you are interested in them, that you want to know what's going on inside their hearts and minds. For a great many people, one of their primary problems is that they simply don't feel heard, and thus don't feel known; you may find that, sometimes, some of the "pressure" of the problem that instigated their visit is actually released simply by their ability to talk through their concerns.

Do not assume you know just what exactly the issue is. Keep asking questions to get deeper. Ask questions that reveal idolatries under sin. As an example, if a man is struggling with pornography use, I ask questions like these:

When did you first see pornography?
How often do you use it?
What kind of pornography do you use?
Why do you think you are drawn to that kind of pornography?
Have you ever been sexually or otherwise physically abused?
In what circumstances do you most feel tempted to use
    pornography?
How do you feel afterwards?
What are your daily spiritual disciplines like?

I ask many more questions besides, but these are the kinds of questions that help get a better sense of the source and spiritual rationale of the sin.

## Validate Feelings without Affirming Assumptions

What people feel is real. It is poor counseling that shames Christians for feeling sad about sad circumstances, angry about legitimately upsetting actions, or anxious about genuinely scary events. A read through the Psalms will only confirm the legitimacy of being honest about our feelings.

And yet you can validate someone's feelings without affirming the assumptions or conclusions they draw about those feelings.

"I feel angry with my husband; therefore, he is obviously sinning against me." The anger is coming from somewhere. We have to talk about it and deal with it. Perhaps her husband is sinning against her, and she has a legitimate grievance with him. Or perhaps her anger is misdirected. Our feelings about others do not always confirm our conclusions about them.

By validating someone's feelings, you give them a safe space to be honest with you and actually process what they're experiencing. By not automatically affirming the judgments they make about the source of these feelings, you give them the spiritual space to evaluate their circumstances and hurts before the Lord and his wisdom in the Word.

## Return Again and Again to the Word of God

The Bible is the fount of wisdom for you and your counselee. If you give advice, connect it to Scripture. Rehearse together the promises of God in Scripture. Remind them of the strong doctrines in Scripture that speak into our fears and anxieties and hurts and grief. Help them discover how healing and satisfying God's Word really is. Ground everything you say and every directive you offer in the eternal wisdom of God in the Bible.

## Refer When Necessary

Pastoral counseling may find you out of your depth of experience and expertise. Remember that pastoral care is actually about people being helped. If you have come to the conclusion that the needs of your member exceed the abilities or wisdom of your church, do not be afraid to refer them to a qualified Christian counselor who may be educated and specifically trained in your area of perceived deficiency.

The kind of counselor to whom you refer will depend on your or your church's particular philosophy of counseling and mental/emotional health care. But do your due diligence in finding capable, competent counseling that you will trust *as a complement to*—not a replacement for—your pastoral care.

I most often refer church members to specialized counselors when they are dealing with significant chemical dependence issues or trauma related to physical or sexual abuse. Another elder or I can continue to meet with them to provide pastoral care, but I have no problem with supplementing this care with the care of one who is exceptionally trained in the area of need. In most cases, with the member's permission, I consult and converse with the other counselor to make sure we are on the same page and unified in our concern and "diagnosis" for the church member.

## Have a Goal in Mind

When you begin counseling sessions, discuss a finish line. You may not set a date for the conclusion of your meetings, but talk over with your member what they want to accomplish, what changes they'd like to see in their life, what habits or skills they think will help, and then work toward those ends.

Nothing can be more discouraging to the pastor and to church members than the counseling sessions that never end. On the flip side, some members will begin to rely unhealthily on the meetings as their means of "getting by" week to week. No real spiritual progress is accomplished, and you simply become the "shot of religion" they feel they need to keep going. If necessary you may, after a sufficient period of time, refer them back to their small group leader or another mature member who can serve as a discipler or mentor for them going forward.

## Don't Promise Confidentiality

Privacy is important, but discern when it is more harmful than helpful. You don't need to let most confessions leave the room, but if there are significant areas of unrepentance that will impact families or the church at large, you do not want to have to violate an unwise promise in keeping others safe.

If a crime is confessed or a sin that impacts others, be responsible to the requisite authorities. You may not live in an area where mandatory reporting of claims of abuse is legally in place, but it is still wise to contact appropriate legal authorities when alerted to a claim of physical or sexual abuse. Your church is not equipped to handle such claims totally in-house. Show deference to potential victims. Even if you doubt the claim actually occurred, do not adjudicate this on your own.

## Remember What Was Said

Remember what people say and, if necessary, take notes (stored securely). There can be few things more demoralizing than meeting with a counselor for the umpteenth time only to have to rehash everything said previously to bring them back up to speed. The feeling begins with not being heard and spreads to sensing a pointlessness to the counseling. Additionally, if there is ever a division or disagreement between you and a counselee over care given and advice offered, having notes gives clarity to your recollection and credence to your understanding of events, should the other elders request an account of your counseling relationship.

## Pray, Pray, Pray

That awkwardness and uneasy silence is an invitation to intercede for the one you're counseling. It is an invitation to ask God to help you. Ask him to give you wisdom, endurance, patience, humility, and warmth. The work of pastoral care is weighty with spiritual power and fraught with potential complications. It is no wonder so many pastors neglect this prayerful drawing near. They much prefer to be on the stage or at the front of the class. But investing time and heart into your flock is how you make your preaching more believable and how you make your leadership more credible. Want to be followed and heeded? Get close and listen.

Even the essence of Christian leadership is made up of a humble followership of Jesus. And we will explore that concept in our next chapter.

## For Reflection

1. What characteristics in another make you feel most heard, understood, and cared for?
2. What are some reasons pastors may underprioritize the work of pastoral care?
3. How would home and hospital visits be received by those in your current ministry context?
4. Why is prayer to God the most important aspect of giving care to others?
5. Why is communicating the gospel essential to effective pastoral care (to those who already ostensibly believe it)?

## For Further Study:

Baxter, Richard. *The Reformed Pastor.* Carlisle, PA: Banner of Truth, 1974.

Baxter, a Puritan, shares biblical thoughts on the "oversight" of a flock that are full of wisdom for those navigating the relational and spiritual challenges of pastoral care. Pay careful attention especially to his treatment of both the pastor's motives and the pastor's manner.

Powlison, David. *Seeing with New Eyes: Counseling and the Human Condition through the Lens of Scripture.* Greensboro, NC: New Growth, 2019.

A must-read for any pastor interested in the ins and outs and practicalities of gospel-centered counseling. If you want to know what it looks and sounds like in the room, how the heart work of grace is translated to actual encounters with needy people, this work is essential.

Sibbes, Richard. *The Bruised Reed.* Carlisle, PA: Banner of Truth, 1998.

This book, while not explicitly on the subject of pastoral care, is still one of the best sources of gracious encouragement and hope for those who suffer, and familiarity with its comforts will serve any pastor exceptionally well.

# CHAPTER 7

# LEADING

The deacons were not happy. We had only recently established a plurality of elders, effectively multiplying my role from one to four, and we had run into our first hitch in the process of sorting out the relationship between the two boards. Naturally, it involved the budget.

In the past, the board of deacons determined a budget proposal to present to the membership for approval. But they had requested a budgetary "vision" from the elders for the upcoming year, one that reflected the pastoral emphases for ministry and mission. From this vision, they planned to craft an official proposal.

The elders interpreted "budgetary vision" as a call to create a sample budget themselves, which they fully expected the deacons to change as needed. It was not the budget proposal, just an idea reflecting the pastoral emphases.

One deacon in particular spoke of the elders' document as being "delivered from on high." He felt dictated to and steamrolled. That was not the elders' intention at all. But it didn't matter. There was a communication breakdown that produced hurt feelings, which led to accusations and bitterness.

I was angry, I confess. As pastor, I had worked with the deacons for several years on the budget process and was used to commiserating with them about the wrong assumptions and second-guessing that occurred in membership meetings about diaconal leadership. Now I was watching them do the same thing to the elders. How could they not see it? I had an opportunity here to rear back and unleash my righteous indignation. I could have called out their unfair assumptions and even their hypocrisy in doing to the new elders what they always grumbled about being done to them by the congregation.

In the moment, I did not want to lead. I wanted to react. To *retort*. Afraid of appearing just as bullheaded as one of our accusers in the meeting, I went the other way. I went into self-protection mode, listening sheepishly and then apologizing. "We obviously misunderstood what you all wanted," I said. "I'm very sorry." It sounds nice, but it was wrong. Just as wrong as it would have been to react in a corresponding anger and let that deacon have it. Why? Because it was a failure to lead pastorally.

The truth is that, biblically speaking, deacons don't direct pastors. My failure to lead well up to this moment had created in the church a kind of bicameral legislature between the pastorate and the diaconate; and since the plurality of elders was new to the process, the diaconate was still acting as de facto elders, as if they could veto elder decisions and directions. This resulted from my inability to anticipate future problems and my unwillingness to exert appropriate authority in the moment.

The "sweet spot" of effective leadership can be very difficult to find. It is no wonder that so few people actually want to be leaders, and no wonder that so few of those who do are able to do it very well. Leadership is intentional influence. Gospel-driven leadership is intentionally influencing others from a heart of grace toward the heart of Christ. This is the kind of leadership sorely lacking among Christian ministers today, including among those most obsessed with leadership as a stand-alone discipline. The leader's heart of grace asks questions like these:

What does leadership centered on the gospel look like in a growing church that is rapidly complexifying?

How do I work the routine management of people and systems without becoming professionalized?

How do I employ the gifts and talents of others in service of our mission without their feeling used and burnt out?

For a ministry driven by the gospel, qualified, called, and commissioned elders must not just hone their leadership skills but also commit to the shaping of their pastoral sensibilities. Pastoring isn't simply religious leadership. The world does not lead like pastors do (or, at least, not as we *should*). For this reason, any discussion of pastoral leadership must return to the pastoral heart.

## Ministry beyond the Minimum

It may not seem like the world of NFL football and the need for pastoral sensibilities go together at all, but there are actually some "intangibles" true of some players that translate quite nicely to what makes up the mettle of more un-rattle-able pastors. I read a book a couple years ago about the world of private quarterback coaching. The book showcased different quarterbacking experts, including NFL veteran Trent Dilfer, who says that there is a rare level of quarterbacking in which players take the bare requirements of talent and athleticism further than everybody else. Dilfer listed now-legendary figures like Peyton Manning and Tom Brady as players who possessed certain "intangibles" that took them above and beyond the others in their field. Dilfer calls these intangibles "the dude qualities" (DQ for short).

DQ according to Dilfer consists of things like being the first one in the facility on practice days, spending more time than required studying game film at home or over late nights at the office, and perhaps more importantly, possessing the mental and emotional tenacity required to "bounce back" after an incredible downturn in a game. When you're down two touchdowns and you just threw an interception, the difference between players like Manning or Brady and everybody else is that they are ready to get back on the field and climb out of the hole. There are some setbacks that don't just take the wind out of a player; they demoralize them such that they are ruined for the rest of the game. They cannot foresee overcoming the apparently insurmountable odds. They see only impossibility, and even with lots of time left on the clock, they give up. But DQ players do not give up until the game is over. They lead even in the midst of adversity. They do not cower or sulk or withdraw. They may be on a losing streak, but they want the ball.

There's a good parallel here for pastors, and really any ministry leaders who are looking to persevere in ministry. If you're interested in longevity (and longsuffering) in ministry, very often the bare minimum of the biblical qualifications is not enough. You need the pastoral "dude qualities."

## Seeing the Whole Field

We've heard numerous times about the advantage of "playing the long game" in ministry. The ability to be patient, to process through potential ramifications of decisions, and to take slow steps before pushing forward on ministry initiatives are all incredibly helpful habits for pastoral work. My own pastor, Nathan Rose, does this really well. I've been very impressed watching him behind the scenes making good, proactive decisions without being rash or simply putting out fires reactively. Nearly any wisdom I have gleaned from pastoral ministry has essentially come from finding the land mines by stepping on them! But very often Nathan has the intuition and relational aptitude to see the land mines and avoid them—or defuse them.

A "next level" pastor is one who is engaged in the trenches and foxholes, yes, but who is also able to keep an eye on the big picture. He measures ramifications of actions. He is not pushed into passivity or impotence by setbacks or negativity; he expects them, assesses them, and factors them into his planning. The pastor who is able to see the whole field isn't afraid to move slowly, think long-term, and in many instances, "detach" from the emotion and anxiety of any given circumstance to think biblically and holistically about ministry decisions. He is not ruled by circumstances but informed by them.

Think of Joseph's long and difficult ministry journey from betrayal by his brothers through slavery to second in command at Pharaoh's court. There must have been times Joseph felt so discouraged he was tempted to despair of life itself. Betrayal, abandonment, and imprisonment will do that to you! But he kept playing the long game. He committed to everyday faithfulness and maintained a vision for the whole field. In the end, when he finally reached a position of power, it didn't go to his head. He was able to stay humble and merciful even from his platform because he didn't get sidetracked from the big picture along the way.

## Resilience

"Affliction produces endurance," writes the apostle Paul (Rom 5:3). The goal is for hardship to contribute to a thick skin, not a hard heart!

So many pastors are "feelers," myself included. We are laid low by conflict, relational tension, insults, or just the general discouragement of ministry troubles. Good pastors centering on the gospel are not unfeeling "bulls in a china shop," of course, but they do see adversity as an opportunity and don't get sidelined by setbacks. They are able to recover from discouragement more enthusiastically and confidently.

Worse than an unfeeling, uncaring pastor is a sullen, whiny, sad-sack pastor. When you're hurt or disappointed, do you tend to retreat into self-pity and lay low? Remember Gideon in the wine-press, avoiding the Midianite fray—the angel of the Lord called him "mighty man of valor." Why? Because the Lord was with him and refused to leave him waiting in the winepress; he was being called into resilience. Even if you are alone or just feel alone, you can take adversity head-on because God is on your side. Get back on the field and go at it. Remember Paul's encouragement to Timothy to "share in suffering like a good soldier of Christ" (2 Tim 2:3).

Ministry is not easy. If it is, you are likely not doing it right. It takes a tender heart and a thick skin, but DQ pastors cultivate resilience.

## Initiative

The truth is, wherever you've followed God's call *to* is where God wants you to lead *from*. Therefore, wherever ministry has taken you, God has appointed you to be the right pastor for that ministry context. You should not expect anyone else to come through the door and do your work for you. No one but you is charged with taking your leadership position or making your leadership decisions.

The apostle James puts a gracious fire under us when he writes, "So it is a sin to know the good and yet not do it." Ouch! Of course, the reason many pastors are passive regarding key leadership decisions is because they fear conflict or the work it might take to avoid it. But the author of Hebrews reminds us:

> For God is not unjust; he will not forget your work and the love you demonstrated for his name by serving the saints—and by continuing to serve them. Now we desire each of you to demonstrate the same diligence for the full assurance of your hope until the end, so that you won't become lazy but will be imitators of those who inherit the promises through faith and perseverance. (Heb. 6:10–12)

In other words, you can repent of laziness, reject passivity, and take initiative because God is on your side! He is not unjust. People may disagree with you, even get angry with you. But your loving service of the saints, however flawed, will be remembered by God. Therefore, you can have all the confidence the allyship of God affords you—and it's a lot!—to move forward in diligence and hope.

Good leaders don't wait for someone else to do their job or make it easier for them to do. They get up, suit up, and do the next right thing (to borrow a phrase from an old pastor of mine). Passivity isn't good for any Christian, but it can be debilitating and toxic for a leader in pastoral ministry. Lead your family, lead your team, lead your church. Be the man God has positioned you uniquely to be. Show initiative.

## Emotional Intelligence

One of the most important DQ's is EQ. Emotional intelligence (or EQ) is one of those intangibles becoming rarer among American pastorates. We like strong personalities, fiery pulpiteers, and theologically rigorous thinkers. And then we're shocked when our leaders say something astoundingly insensitive or relationally stupid. We're surprised when they don't know how to speak to a man struggling with same-sex attraction or what to do for a woman struggling in a verbally abusive marriage. Emotionally stunted or stupid pastors are awkward around people's feelings, squeamish around people's hurts, and unsympathetic to people's fears.

This is why we must insist that our pastors actually be *pastors*, with preacher-theologian as a subset of that office. Low EQ pastors do untold damage because they see the church as an audience or a followership not as a flock to be cared for.

Think of Paul speaking about having an open heart with those he ministers to (2 Cor 6:11). Consider the nurturing image in his comparing ministry to the breastfeeding of babies (1 Thess 2:7). He had a deeply felt "concern" for the churches (2 Cor 11:28) born of Christ's own compassion (Matt 9:36).

Some may say this is really a feature of personality type—extroversion or introversion and the like. But personality type has almost no bearing on this. Many introverted pastors are great in counseling, visitation, and personal discipleship scenarios, and many extroverted pastors are terrible. And vice versa. It's not about introversion versus extroversion—it's about emotional intelligence, the ability to empathize, relate, and connect.

The bottom line is that if you do not love people, you ought not be a pastor. And this means actually loving them, not simply loving what people do for you or enjoying the attention of a crowd. A real "people person" may, nevertheless, be very low in EQ, because enjoying being with people is not the same as enjoying people. Real love is an others-orientation in which one listens, relates, and seeks to understand.

Pastor, you must *actually love* people, not just love how they make you feel.

## Leading Yourself

You cannot effectively lead others if you do not conscientiously lead yourself. The pastor who is subject to his week, who routinely has ministry "happen" to him, is not evidencing the fruit of self-control or the spirit of discipline.

Pastors should take inventory of their weekly schedules. Does it reveal that we say yes (or no) to too much? Does it show that we are disorganized people, always playing catch-up?

Do you devote time not just to study God's Word, but to read books—theology, spirituality, history, biography, even fiction and poetry? Do you stretch yourself in your reading, working different mental and emotional muscles? Do you go to conferences or access other resources for pastors that might challenge and inspire you?

It's a cliché, of course, but it's a cliché because it's true: leaders are learners.

In your personal relationships, do you stew, grumble, and internally process to the exclusion of other's needs to talk and listen? Would your wife or closest friends say you're great with communication? Do you manage your household well?

The answers to these questions help reveal the quality of your self-leadership. Even more telling is your commitment to the spiritual disciplines of Bible study, prayer, fasting, service, and generosity. For the same reason we should dismiss the gluttonous preacher who rails against others' lack of self-control; the pastor who does not show personal discipline and commitment should not expect others to follow his leadership. "Be imitators of me, as I am of Christ," Paul says (1 Cor 11:1 ESV). To be a good leader, one must be a good follower. To be a gospel-driven leader, one must first be an attentive follower of the heart of Jesus.

I have had numerous discussions with ministry leaders about why it's so difficult to find truly gospel-centered leadership. Oh, there are a multitude of leaders who admire or otherwise identify with the gospel-centered paradigm. They read books on the subject (maybe even this one), frequent the right websites, attend the right conferences, listen to the right podcasts, and travel in the right circles. But when the leadership rubber meets the ministry road, they do not strike those who serve under them as particularly ruled by the gospel. They even struggle to preach in gospel-centered ways. How does this happen?

I suspect that many who lack the aroma of Christ in their leadership actually lack the aroma of Christ in their spiritual lives. They have probably gotten so accustomed to the routine of ministry that the Scriptures and the Christ within them have become more a matter of feeding others rather than feeding themselves. The Bible has become something dealt out without first being something dwelled in.

At the inaugural Gospel Coalition Conference in 2007, Tim Keller gave the seminal talk "What Is Gospel-Centered Ministry?"—the message that contains the now-classic "Jesus is the true and better" application. At the end of that homiletical run, Keller said something that has stuck with me ever since I first heard it. He said, "That's not typology; that's an instinct."[1] Of course, what Keller was doing *was* typology. But I think what he meant was that Christ-centered preachers can hardly help but preach Christ. They would have to make themselves avoid preaching the gospel. If anything, the temptation is to "jump over" the immediate exposition of the text to, as Spurgeon famously said, "make a road to Christ."

In other words, if we are regularly communing with Christ, reading the Scriptures devotionally in a daily and disciplined way, and praying without ceasing (1 Thess 5:17), the instincts of grace will be natural—which is to say *supernatural*. It is a Spiritual impulse that "organically" finds its way into our sermon preparation. How could a gospel-centered preacher not preach a gospel-centered sermon? How could a leader *actually centered on the gospel* not lead in a gospel-centered way? Perhaps the reason so many pastors who engage in all the right gospel stuff still struggle to lead in gospel patterns is because they are not in regular communion with the Christ who is the center of the gospel.

## Personal Discipleship

The first leadership strategy of the gospel-driven pastor is not to manage systems or to build brand recognition, but personally to help other people follow Jesus. Discipleship is, in fact, the proper mission of the church. Our perfect Leader mandated, then, to his followers that they lead in making other followers.

---

1. Timothy Keller, "What Is Gospel-Centered Ministry?" (sermon, The Gospel Coalition Conference, Chicago, May 23, 2007), https://www.thegospelcoalition.org/conference_media/gospel-centered-ministry/.

If pastors do not lead in this regard, how in the world could they expect their congregation to be about this business? If you don't make disciples, pastor, do not be shocked if your church struggles to make disciples. Set an example to the flock in replicating follow-ership of Jesus, of passing on the faith, and you will set the tone for a discipling church serious about the Great Commission.

Below I share some pointers on the pastor's personal disciple making. Putting these ideas into practice will help you understand the goal and enjoy the process (and fruit!) of discipleship.

## Disciple in Proximity

If you look back in your life, who has made the biggest difference in your relationship with Jesus? I think of two men in particular in my life, both my youth pastors at different times. Christ Trent let me tag along when I was just a middle school kid as he went on evangelism trips to downtown Albuquerque. He had me into his home for family meals. I watched how he spoke to and cared for his wife. I watched how he parented his kids. Mike Ayers was my youth pastor when I was in high school, and I later became the youth pastor at his church plant. He let me hang out in his office. He took me to lunch. He asked for my feedback on ideas and ministry objectives. These men let me into their routines, into their spheres of being. I learned a lot from our talks, but I also learned a lot simply by watching.

Odds are, the person who has had the greatest impact on your walk with Jesus is someone with whom you actually had a relationship. Authors and celebrity preachers may have influenced you, but it is likely that the most significant impact you've experienced has come from the up-close interaction with a relative, a friend, or a church leader. When conducted biblically, personal discipleship looks a lot like friendship.

In a way, everything in a church is "discipleship," but the impact of spiritual growth is experienced more greatly in proximity.

## Disciple with Priority

Personal proximity is essential to discipleship, but the pastor cannot personally disciple everyone—not even everyone who desires such an arrangement with him. Therefore, he will need to prioritize whom he disciples and for how long.

It is important for pastors to prioritize those more mature in their faith, under the assumption that newer believers can benefit from discipling relationships with those just a bit further along than them. Ideally, anyone who's been a Christian for more than a couple of years should be capable of working with a new believer to go through a book on sound doctrine or the spiritual disciplines or discuss parts of Scripture. But more mature believers need one further along than themselves to speak into their lives. Typically, those qualified in church leadership are among the few who fit that bill. In your eagerness to shepherd new believers along their spiritual journey, don't neglect more established Christians who could benefit from your time. They will likely slip through the cracks.

At the same time, if you can manage it, discipling a new or immature believer can be an extremely rewarding experience for both of you. In your case, it can be refreshing and encouraging to see the faith with new eyes. The eagerness and wonder of new believers can supply great energy for seasoned pastors and add a special relatability and intuition to their preaching.

In some cases, you may want to meet with more than one man for discipleship at a time, perhaps in twos or threes, or even in a men's discipleship group. Aside from preaching, this was my favorite part of pastoral ministry. In my last church, I met one-on-one with two men about once a month. One was a more immature believer, and the other was more mature and a potential elder candidate. My approach with each was different. But I also led a men's discipleship group twice a month on Monday nights. In that venue, we had about twelve men going through book discussions and having confessional conversations. These were my discipling priorities, and the fruit was in these men's ability both to love their neighbors well and to disciple other men accordingly.

## Disciple Personally

Remember that discipleship is not merely about information but about character. You are training someone in the faith, which can—and will—involve working through the Scriptures to establish soundness of doctrine. Following Jesus necessitates knowing more about him. But the work of discipleship is not purely about knowledge but about knowledge that transforms. Thus, you should not be afraid to get personal at key points.

Ask personal questions of those you are discipling with increased frequency and depth. Ask about their sins, about their fears, about their fruit. Don't just assume they're doing well and go through the motions of your book discussion or group habits. Dig down deep to provide accountability and encouragement. Remember that gospel-driven pastors care more about others' sanctification than their own success.

# Four Components of Gospel-Driven Leadership

I have previously shared some of the pastoral "dude qualities" that make up the *disposition* of good leadership. Here, I want to share some hallmarks of leadership *practice*. As with every other subject in this book, there is a lot more that can and should be said, but I have prioritized the following four components of gospel-driven leadership.

## Decisiveness

Pastors overly concerned about their own protection or reputation will grow passive over time. The "bull in a china shop" pastor is not your only alternative, however. Gospel confidence, as discussed previously, rightly leads to leaders taking initiative. When you know who you are in Christ and adequately meditate on your union with him (and thus your security in him), you will be bold to take appropriate leadership steps.

No one else is called to do this for your church. If you consistently let those who are not in leadership positions take initiative, they become the real leaders, not you. Do not be afraid to be decisive. Pray much. Mull things over, consult with others, research, then think, and think, and think. But passivity is part of the original sin. Avoid analysis paralysis, and don't always be afraid of making mistakes. You're going to make them, even if you take forever to do so. If your church has affirmed your calling to lead, then *lead*. The grace of Christ frees you to operate with boldness.

## Responsibility

Bad leaders shift blame. Good leaders take responsibility. If we are happy to receive credit when things go right but are always passing the buck when things go wrong, we have implicitly prioritized our glory over God's.

We do not like to lead others who are constantly making excuses, so why engage in this lazy practice ourselves? If we want others to be responsible for their decisions, we must set the tone by taking appropriate ownership of ours. There is nothing anybody can say about us that will nullify God's approval of us in Jesus. So, don't be afraid to confess sin, to accept the fault, and to self-evaluate when those you're leading may be reproducing your bad habits or deficient leadership style.

## Humility

Not only is humility a great adornment to Christian leadership; without it, the pastor disqualifies himself. Love is not proud or arrogant. The gospel-driven pastor, out of love for his flock, does not need to exert his control over them, to dress down those who make mistakes, to condemn those who sin, or to denigrate those who don't measure up.

In this regard, it is good to keep an eye on the level of sarcasm or "sizing up" that takes place in our leadership cultures. Good-natured ribbing can be fun among brothers, but in some contexts it becomes a means of power and positioning. Those under our leadership may not experience our sarcastic comments or jokes as brotherly affection at all. Power differences have significant effects.

Don't feel as though you must always have your way or the last word. Be the first to admit failures. Be open to constructive criticism. Give permission for others to disagree without repercussion. And don't think so much of your own position and power as you do the presence of Christ.

Christ came to us meek and lowly. Gospel-driven leadership, then, is not really about being the one over others calling the shots but about being the one out in front taking the hits. Point others to Jesus by embracing the humility of Jesus (Phil 2:5–8).

## Delegation

Hunger for power doesn't always look like arrogance and abuse. Sometimes it looks like fear and passivity. The leader confident in the gospel will free others to lead according to their gifts and maturity. The pastor who is trying to do everything himself, whether out of personal control or "quality control" concerns, has an idolatry problem.

Equipping and releasing others to help is part of the remedy. The body is made up of parts, and the Lord's numerous gifts to the church exist to make sure the glory goes to him, not to leaders. One of the most important components of Christian leadership is the passing of the baton to others, the developing and empowering of others to replicate and increase the work of ministry. Don't be afraid to delegate to others. Think of it, in fact, as essential to good leadership. You can't and shouldn't be doing it all.

And if you are struggling to find others to whom you might delegate some work, it might mean that either the work itself is not necessary (perhaps not at the scale from which you are trying to carry it out) or that you need to implement a process to develop other leaders to help carry the load.

## Leadership Development

The pastor's development of other leaders should be a vital aspect of his disciple-making strategy. Whether it's the mutual sharpening taking place among elders or personal discipleship of a man aspiring to the office, every pastor should be thinking as early as he can about raising up the next generation of faithful shepherds and even of passing his own baton to an eventual successor.

Do not shepherd out of a concern for your own kingdom. Be thinking about discipleship deficits in your church and the missional needs around your region and even the ends of the earth. You cannot solve every problem through your ministry, but you can contribute to the raising of the next army of gospel-loving saints by starting where you are with whatever you have.

For many pastors of lesser-resourced churches, this may simply entail personal discipleship that is intentionally aimed at creating an on-ramp to eldership. Other pastors should seriously consider developing pastoral residency programs and ministry internships, funding and facilitating seminary education or other training, and abundantly resourcing all the people in your church in the areas of Bible teaching and spiritual disciplines. It takes time, of course, to intentionally develop leaders in your church, but it doesn't have to cost a lot of money, and the investment will be one that pays off abundant dividends in the ministry's future.

My previous church was small and rural. There were not a lot of young men around who cared anything about ministry. I took it upon myself both to disciple the few young men who showed interest personally, but also to develop a residency program by which aspiring pastors could get a sense of rural ministry by serving for a time at my side. It was largely an informal relationship, but it was also intensive and personal. We only had one resident, but do not despise the day of small beginnings.

In my current context, I lead a residency program that is more formal, and yet still heavily discipleship based. The program runs for eighteen months and up to twelve young men at a time serve within it. We meet once a month as a group to discuss our monthly reading and writing. We work through sessions with attendant readings on gospel-centrality, biblical theology, pastoral care, preaching, worship, membership, and the like. We conduct two preaching labs. But the heart of the program is one-on-one discipleship, spending time with each man over coffee and meals. Some travel with me to speaking engagements.

The whole enterprise is built around pouring into the next generation of pastors, that they can be equipped in the gospel as much as possible and serve their churches humbly and powerfully. I am not an old man (yet), but I want to take this transition seriously. If I were not committed to leadership development in my personal ministry, I think my public ministry could legitimately be considered self-serving. We must be serious about leadership development because by spending our time and energy and resources on it, we serve and demonstrate our love for the future church.

What you may discover also is that having any formal plan for leadership development in place, no matter how small the scale, makes your church a magnet for maturing believers. Aspiring leaders go where they know they will be discipled and trained.

## Leading Change

The most common leadership conundrum facing pastors is how to lead change in a church in a gracious but effective way. People are hard changers, and Christians who are accustomed to the comfortability and familiarity of their church homes especially so. Add to this dynamic the spiritualizing of "the way it's always been," and any leader interested in directing significant change in a congregation has his work cut out for him! Many a new pastoral hire has cut short his tenure through an ill-timed or ill-executed plan of change.

Think of any change as a potential expense of relational capital or the spending of credibility. The larger the change envisioned, the more it may cost; thus, you want to give enough time to have "saved up" enough to make a major change. Space out the changes you would like to make. Churches can suffer "change fatigue," which can easily become disgruntlement or bitterness against leadership if they are not given enough time to recover. Below are some further keys to leading change in a gracious way, adapted from an earlier work, *The Gospel-Driven Church*. (For a fuller exploration of these principles, consult chapter 10 of that book.)

## Take It Personally but Don't Make It Personal

In other words, own the change you want to make. Be convictional about it. Don't just change for change's sake. "Shaking things up" as a leadership style has almost nothing to do with biblical pastoral ministry. So, make sure you have good theological and philosophical reasons for the change you want to make. But don't take it personally when some question or hesitate. Don't turn resistance to change into a pretense for drawing lines and stoking division.

## Practice the Spiritual Fruit of Patience

As you lead others out of their comfort zones or propose other changes that challenge their long-held traditions, have abundant patience for their discomfort or confusion. The more significant the change, the more patience you should ask the Lord to give you.

## Move Slowly and Strategically

Don't make a lot of big changes at once, if you can help it. Pick your battles carefully. Seek to build consensus. Help others feel like they are a part of the movement, not simply that the change is happening *to* them.

The new pastor, for instance, may assume his office with a long list of ideas and programs he would like to implement—or a long list of those he would like to end. My advice to recent hires of an existing church is not to make any unnecessary changes of significance for a while. Your being new is a big enough change for the church for the time being. Let the congregation get to know you and acclimate to your leadership. This also allows you to gain wisdom in how to lead others you don't know very well at first. The new pastor can avoid many transition landmines by slowing down and investing in building relational capital with the church.

## Show Meekness and Give Mercy

Do not push. Lead. Be gracious with those who struggle with change. Don't chastise them. Don't be passive-aggressive about them from the pulpit. Listen well. Afford people all the grace you would want if someone was doing something new you didn't understand or agree with.

## Employ Plurality and Embrace Parity

The benefit of multiple pastors cannot be overstated. It is best that a significant change be represented as the vision of the *pastors*, plural. If you are a solo pastor, seek to build consensus from the leaders you have available. If this is limited to only laypersons influential in the congregation, spend time with them and explain what you want to do and why. Seek to get them on board and solicit their wisdom. Let it be seen as a group project not a single prerogative.

## Overcommunicate

Much confusion can be alleviated by simply reiterating the need for the change in many venues and at many times. You are probably not in danger of communicating it too much. Most church folks only think about church stuff when Sundays roll around. They are not spending their weeks reading, praying, studying, and planning like you are. Do your best to bring them up to speed.

## Show Your Cards

Be transparent. Be honest. Don't just share the what; explain the why. Explain the reason for changes and detail exactly how you expect them to be implemented.

## Operate Consistently

Don't "pick on" one segment of the church's sacred cows while leaving others' unaddressed. For instance, fixating on rehabilitating what you perceive as a poorly run women's discipleship program without addressing men's discipleship or other areas can give the false impression that you are targeting women. The most common scenario where this kind of discrimination can be perceived is in the handling of senior programs. Focusing on programs only involving older saints, for example, often feels callous and plays into congregational fears of idolizing youth or "putting old folks out to pasture." But any inconsistent application of programmatic change can come off as showing partiality. So communicate clearly and be consistent in what you do.

## Celebrate Wins

Be your church's chief cheerleader and encourager. This is hugely important for gospel-driven leadership generally not just the leading of change. Make it your duty to serve and build up others, stoking their joy in the Lord. Don't always focus on what isn't done or what hasn't been done correctly. Be a champion of your church's happiness. Honor other leaders publicly and privately. Thank the church when changes are successfully implemented. Celebrate with others when any advancement is made, and shift the credit for successes to others.

## Keep Preaching the Gospel

Do not let your desire for change overshadow your core commitment to proclaiming the gospel. Keep the main thing the main thing, and do not make an idol of your visions for growth or congregational transformation.

There is a lot more to know and do when it comes to leading gracious change in a church, and a lot will depend on your knowledge, the extent of your tenure, and your church's size, age, and context. Christian leadership is not about a formula. Handy lists of principles like those above do not ensure that everything will always go well. There are always dozens of factors and thousands of contingencies that make Christian leadership as much a matter of discernment and prudence as anything else. Remember to *pastor* through any changes.

# The Importance of the Pastoral "I Don't Know"

Sometimes leadership is not about dispensing wisdom. Actually, it's *mostly* not! One of the most valuable sentences in a pastor's arsenal is "I don't know." The honest admission "I don't know" is an important leadership skill that we must learn.

The pressure to know and be everything everybody expects us to know and be can be pride-puffing. I once worked at a Christian bookstore where we were told never to say "I don't know" to a customer. We must give them some answer, any answer, even if it was a guess or likely even a wrong answer. Customers don't want to hear "I don't know" from service people, but even a wrong answer makes them feel helped. I confess that the temptation to satisfy the customer has persisted through my ministry days for a variety of reasons. I want people to feel helped. And I also don't like looking like a rube. Why is it important for pastors to say "I don't know" when, indeed, they don't?

## "I Don't Know" Is Often the Truth

First and foremost, if you don't know the answer to something, say you don't know the answer. Making stuff up is not our calling. We all know some folks who seem pathologically unable to admit ignorance in any area. Don't trust those people. Better a disappointing truth than a manipulative or misleading fabrication.

## "I Don't Know" Impresses the Right People

I've done more than a few Q&As after preaching or on panels at speaking engagements before, and the desire to impress with wisdom and insight can be nerve-wracking. Once, during a Q&A after a sermon in my church planting days, I got really honest when a question stumped me. I don't remember what it was, but I remember realizing I had no information available to my brain to even begin formulating a halfway intelligent response. I just said, "I'm sorry, but I don't know the answer to that." Afterwards, a young lady who was not a believer approached me to express her appreciation for my honesty. She said she wished more religious people could admit when they don't know, too.

The reality is that acting like you know everything impresses shallow, naive, or otherwise easily impressed people. But saying "I don't know" impresses people who value honesty and appreciate their pastor admitting weakness, ignorance, or just general fallibility.

## "I Don't Know" Trains Others Not to Be Know-It-Alls

Once a fellow came up to me after our worship service to ask about the Old Testament figure Ahimelech. I recognized the name but could not recall his biblical importance or the narrative where he was found. My inquirer expected that, as a pastor, I would know all about this figure and even the references where he would be found. I blanked. When I looked him up later, of course I "remembered" who Ahimelech was, but in the moment, despite the prospect of losing face with a relatively new Christian, I said, "Brother, I don't remember. I just don't know." This led to a great talk about so-called "Bible trivia," knowledge, learning, wisdom, righteousness, and the like.

I think it was a teachable moment for both of us, but I walked away believing that when a leader is open about the gaps in his knowledge, it trains others to be okay with not knowing everything. Of course, we want to know our Bibles as well as we possibly can, but we want to remember that knowledge puffs up and that the Scriptures and the doctrines they teach are meant to make us full-hearted with Christ—not big-headed with minutiae.

## "I Don't Know" Cultivates Pastoral Humility

It is good for a pastor's heart—no matter the reception—to make his *I don't know* public. This admission shapes our selflessness and helps us become less self-conscious and more self-aware, and it conforms us more to the humility of Christ. And humility, remember, is a core component of gospel-driven leadership.

The truth is that pastoral leadership is not all it's cracked up to be. Many training for ministry envision only the perks of the office, the renown of the pulpit. But pastoral leadership takes us into the mud and muck of human relationships, into the complicated and often chaotic world of congregational life. To lead well demands dependence on the spirit of discernment and careful navigation between conflict and an elusive peace. It's to this delicate navigation that we will now turn our focus.

## For Reflection

1. Think of a time from your past when you felt you were really growing in extraordinary ways. Who was most influential in your discipleship at that time? How did they influence you?
2. What are some barriers to your own practice of personal discipleship?

3. What strengths and weaknesses characterize your own sense of leadership? What is your plan to develop in the areas of your weakness?

4. Describe your own pastoral plan to nurture a culture of discipleship and leadership development in your church.

5. In what specific ways does the gospel keep a pastor from having to be his church's all-knowing messiah? What does it say to the pastor in this regard? To the flock?

## For Further Study:

Miller, C. John. *The Heart of a Servant Leader: Letters from Jack Miller.* Phillipsburg, NJ: P&R, 2004.

> This collection of letters was assembled after Jack Miller's death and reflects the depths of grace he is known for and provides ample evidence as to why he's considered the spiritual father of many influential ministers today. Miller's insights into the heart of leadership reveal the very heart of Christ.

Sanders, J. Oswald. *Spiritual Leadership: A Commitment to Excellence for Every Believer.* 4th ed. Chicago: Moody Publishers, 2007.

> While not intended solely for ministers, this biblical treatment of leadership from the former director of the China Inland Mission is still (rightly) considered an essential work on the subject.

Spurgeon, Charles Haddon. *The Soul Winner: How to Lead Sinners to the Saviour.* Grand Rapids: Eerdmans, 1989.

> This surprisingly lengthy treatise on evangelism is actually full of insightful thoughts on beginning and leading a culture of discipleship in a church.

# CHAPTER 8

# FIGHTING (AND MAKING PEACE)

I could tell that the man on the other end of the phone felt at the end of his rope. He was one of the younger guys in the ministry cohort I coach, and I had already sensed his exasperation in the email requesting the call. He was just four years into his pastorate, and he was dealing with some really difficult things. Over the phone, I asked him to describe the situation.

"Well," he said, "I inherited these deacons who've been doing things the same way for thirty years, and they are really reluctant to make changes. They seem like they're listening to me, but then they ignore what I suggest. There's this older guy in the church who's the patriarch of a big family with multiple members in the church, and he seems to have the most influence; I've been told if I disappoint him, he could take them all out with him, and we'd lose a lot of giving. And I have these ladies who run a few programs that are really outdated, and nobody attends them except themselves. It's more of a fellowship for them than any kind of service to the church or the community, and I'm stressed about how to suggest discontinuing them. And there's a couple of guys who come up to me every Sunday after I preach to offer me pointers and little critiques. One of them, I know, has started sharing his criticism with others in the church, and I don't know if it constitutes a gossip or divisiveness situation or not. And, on top of it all, there are one or two ladies who are being very passive-aggressive to my wife."

I listened to all this, and I said, "Brother, you know what it sounds like to me?"

"What?" he said.

I said, "It sounds like you've got a church."

What my friend had finally experienced was the reality of his church. The honeymoon period of the first couple of years was over. For a while, he was new. They liked his wife and thought his kids were cute. They smiled at his new ideas and enjoyed his preaching. People were on their best behavior. Then they got tired of holding up the front. And they realized he was actually serious about the stuff he was saying.

It's usually about year three or four that a new pastor actually discovers what church he's pastoring. It's rarely the one shown to him throughout the search process. It is a lot like marriage on the day we stop trying to impress each other and suddenly become our real selves. This is usually when marriage troubles begin. We are shocked—shocked!—that we have married a sinner. And so are they. A similar thing happens in new pastorates.

The truth is that most of these issues, as painful and trying as they can be, can be endured and even prevailed over. Most pastors I know who have been in the same place for more than fifteen years are able to look back at the moment the church "got real." At the time, they wondered if they should leave. Perhaps they weren't called to this church, after all. But they stayed. They stayed faithful in the midst of conflict and confusion. And on the backside of it all, their ministries took on new resonance and they experienced new joy.

Doubting one's call in the midst of difficulty is a common temptation for every pastor. Sometimes, the Lord truly is calling us elsewhere. (Many times, he does it in times of peace, which can be just as challenging.) But the main reason we question our calling in times of difficulty is because we have a false assumption about the nature of ministry. Where in the Bible do we see any indication that if God calls us to something, it will be easy or comfortable?

Pastor, do not immediately equate a difficult ministry with a lack of calling. It is quite likely that God, in his wisdom, has chosen exactly you for exactly this moment. He has stewarded *this* church, with all of its problems, *to you*. And in such cases, he is not calling you away, but calling you *into* the chaos. He is calling you to fight.

## Three Primary Battles

This fight for faithfulness is not *against* your people but *for* them. It is not advisable that you pick a fight with anyone in your church. Remember that the Bible forbids pastors being "quarrelsome" (1 Tim 3:3). The pastor who is always spoiling for a fight will always do damage to his church in other ways, as this demeanor is reflective of one who is a poor repenter, a poor receiver of the fruit of the Spirit. There are many times when the church's shepherds must address unrepentant sin or conflict within the congregation, and I will speak to those shortly, but that is primarily a field of peace. The fields of ministerial wars are largely unseen. We fight on three primary battlegrounds against three often underestimated opponents.

### Against the Enemy

Several years ago, a pastor friend had visited me at my church, and I was relaying to him some trouble I'd been having with anxiety attacks while driving. The episodes had just begun a few months previous, and I was struggling to understand why. I had been driving for nearly two decades by then and had never had any problems.

Now I found myself suffering from flashes of panic while driving on interstates or in bad weather conditions. My friend said, "Have you considered it as a demonic attack?"

I confess I had not. I was thinking mostly about stress in my life, about diet and exercise. It had not occurred to me to think that these attacks could be the result of the actions of evil spirits. To this day, I am not convinced that they were. But I was chastened, nevertheless, because my friend reminded me of something I too easily forget. The devil is real, and he hates pastors.

In his passage on the qualifications for the pastorate, Peter sounds the warning:

> Be sober-minded; be watchful. Your adversary the devil prowls around like a roaring lion, seeking someone to devour. Resist him, firm in your faith, knowing that the same kinds of suffering are being experienced by your brotherhood throughout the world. (1 Peter 5:8–9 ESV)

Peter knew firsthand the designs Satan has on God's servants. The enemy knows if he wants to destroy a church, the best door of entry is the leadership.

Knowing this is not meant to make us timid or anxious—quite the opposite. We are stewarded the powerful gospel of Jesus Christ. The devil's doom is sure. Indeed, "one little word shall fell him."[1] But awareness is a lot of the battle. Do not let your guard down. Keep your head on a swivel. Stay alert to the reality of the spiritual forces of wickedness. They are daily conspiring against your ministry and against your church. It may not be adultery that is most likely to lure you, but any disqualifying sin will constitute moral failing enough.

Therefore, fight the devil by fighting for joy in the Lord. When you are extra vulnerable, be extra vigilant to feed on God's Word.

---

1. "A Mighty Fortress," words by Martin Luther (1529).

Pray for God's strength to shield you. Pray earnestly that God would keep you from temptation and deliver you from evil. The devil wants to see you fail. Spite him and fight him.

## Against the Self

Perhaps the greatest battle you will face will be the one against your own tendencies to sloth, gluttony, and pride. Every pastor is lazy about *something*. For some, it is the work of theological study. For others, it is spending time with the sheep. For some, it is being patiently attentive to the high-maintenance state of the congregation. For others, it is directly addressing problems in a timely and decisive fashion. The pendulums swing hard both ways. In the midst of difficult pastorates, the drifts toward bitterness or self-pity are always a danger. Even just dwelling on our own hurt feelings or grievances is entering into a rough surf of discontent, the current of which can drag us far out to sea and drown us. The pastor's worst enemy is usually himself. No critic will be more withering. No admirer will be more inflating. No sinner will be more demoralizing.

Peter exhorts elders this way, "Humble yourselves, therefore, under the mighty hand of God so that at the proper time he may exalt you, casting all your anxieties on him, because he cares for you" (1 Peter 5:6–7 ESV). The pursuit of humility will require a daily onslaught of Godward disciplines and attitudes. Begin with centering yourself on God's Word. Embrace the posture of humility by praying your guts out—"casting all your anxieties on him."

Jesus warns us: "If anyone would come after me, let him deny himself and take up his cross daily and follow me" (Luke 9:23 ESV). The work of ministry is a work of daily crucifixion of self. You set aside your preferences, your comfort, and your safety for the edification of the saints. The trade-off is that those who die to themselves will discover a joy and satisfaction they would not otherwise experience. No laziness or gluttony can fulfill like Christ. No pursuit of selfish ambition or self-centered dreaming will satisfy like getting to the end of a hard period of shepherding God's people and realizing that, by his grace, you stayed humble, faithful, and peaceful.

This will be the fight of your life.

## Against the Wolves

The pastor must daily be fighting his flesh and waging war against the powers and principalities of darkness. But, occasionally, another kind of opposition enters the church. Not the ordinary kind of disbelief or spiritual apathy, this opposition is subtle but intentional. It is set on disruption and division.

The Good Shepherd gives this warning to the flock: "Beware of false prophets, who come to you in sheep's clothing but inwardly are ravenous wolves" (Matt 7:15 ESV). This is not a warning primarily about unbelievers, who are goats in Jesus's pastoral metaphor. Goats are not sheep, to be sure, but goats can and should be entreated to believe and loved as best as possible—not to the neglect of the sheep but in the way of compassionate concern. Wolves are different. Goats and sheep can mingle (and do every week at your church). Wolves are set on the destruction of the flock (Acts 20:29).

The man I told you about before, the heretic I kicked out of my church—he was a wolf. But sometimes, the wolf is not an outsider who's wandered in. Sometimes they are insiders showing their true fur. You've pushed this grace stuff too far. You really do intend for the church to be serious about mission. You've upset business as usual, and you're seeing the fangs.

Not every critic is a wolf! Critical believers can be reasoned with. If you disagree on a point of tertiary doctrine or a leadership decision, peace can be found, even if agreement cannot. True believers who disagree with each other can still coexist in harmony, because the Christ they have in common is more precious to them. The process of peace may take a long time (again, see the discussion below), but these critics are not unrepentantly seeking the harm of the body. Don't confuse every critic for a wolf.

But wolves are real. And whether they are trying to sow false doctrine or influence others toward sin, their aim is disruption and division of the body. Paul warns Titus: "As for a person who stirs up division, after warning him once and then twice, have nothing more to do with him, knowing that such a person is warped and sinful; he is self-condemned" (Titus 3:10–11 ESV). The fight against wolves must be intentional and direct. Why? Because you love the sheep. Because you want to protect the sheep.

One of the biggest regrets I have from my time in pastoral ministry was my passivity when facing the sowing of division and gossip within the body. I met with the divisive persons to appeal to their profession of faith and try to sort out their grievance, even apologizing if necessary. But the divisiveness persisted. I did not obey the Bible's instructions on divisive persons (Rom 16:17; Titus 3:10). I feared creating unnecessary disputations in the church. I feared being misunderstood. And, in general, I just feared conflict. And the result was that I let the disease fester. The church would have been better off going through whatever radical impact disciplining the wolves would have made at the time. A temporary wound is always worth it on the way to peace. And obeying God is always worth a temporary wound.

My friend Ray once told me that in sticky issues of church discipline, "Sometimes we have to protect certain people from the church. And sometimes we have to protect the church from certain people." If you want to protect the flock God has called you to pastor, you will answer the call to fight wolves no matter the cost.

These are primary fields of battle for the pastor himself. But there is frequently conflict among the professing members of the church. Many pastors, in fact, find themselves like the young man from my coaching group, neck-deep in hostile territory he did not anticipate. The important thing to remember there is that the pastoral impulse should not be toward contributing to the conflict but pacifying it. There are important things to fight for in our churches, but our end goal should be to establish peace. To get there, we have to understand what is often really going on in the midst of hostility.

## Making Sense of Hostility

Conflict is many pastors' Achilles' heel. Some overcompensate in impatience and anger. Others underaddress in passivity and timidity.

Pastoral ministry frequently feels like a Sisyphean ordeal, eternally pushing a rock up a hill only for it to roll down again. You get to the end of three months counseling someone, and they don't seem any further helped than they did when they first walked in. You may feel the lament of Ecclesiastes, "Vanity of vanities, says the Preacher, vanity of vanities! All is vanity" (1:2 ESV).

You may preach on unity and the bonds of peace on Sunday morning and then that very Sunday evening walk into a members' meeting that feels like a scene from the wild west.

You may get to the office on Monday morning, exhausted, stressed, bleary-eyed, and ready to push that rock back up the hill, only to find that all that water you parted the previous day has rushed back into place. You may be staring at your email inbox and seeing your voicemail notifications and looking at that calendar of appointments for the week and that blank sheet of paper where the next Sunday's sermon is supposed to be and think it all a chasing of the wind (Eccl 2:11).

You may feel "all is vanity." Especially when you are ministering in the midst of conflict, division, unfair or undue criticism, or even hostility. All your faithful preaching, your patient listening, your un-self-defensive absorption of personal slights and insinuations don't seem to earn you much credit. The more a martyr you're willing to be, the more they seem willing to make you one. No one is impressed by your passive acceptance of their insults and maneuvering against you.

Ecclesiastes 7 is, of course, not directly a text on pastoral ministry, much less enduring hostility in the midst of it. However, I believe the Teacher has a word we can apply for the work. Below are four important words on shepherding in the midst of hostility.

## Hostility Is Clarifying

Hostility is clarifying, but that does not mean the hostility itself is easy to understand. Sometimes the most confusing, confounding thing to understand in ministry is why people are so angry.

One thing you can't quite prepare for, and that is as profoundly hurtful as it is confusing, is that you will have people in your church who just don't like you for apparently no reason. This is really one of the weirdest parts of pastoral ministry, and maybe the most unfortunate. When you're a pastor, you discover that you disappoint some people just by *being*. You're not enough *something* for some, or you're too much of *something else* for others.

    a. I always did my best to ask how or why I had offended someone or what had come between us, but some people can't give a reason (or won't). This is always frustrating. And when it resulted in hard treatment of my wife, it was angering. But I never could quite get used to pastoring people who could not or would not explain why they were rude, disruptive, or divisive.

There can definitely be a *lack* of clarity in the hostility. But the *existence* of it is clarifying—about your role, your position. Hostility—and difficulty, conflict, and pain in general—is clarifying about where you stand, about *what you're there to do*. Suffering is a kind of mineral spirits for the pastor, stripping away all the varnish of our self-sufficiency and our illusions about what pastoral ministry is, what we're *for*.

The Teacher writes in Ecclesiastes 7:1–4,

> A good name is better than precious ointment,
>> and the day of death than the day of birth.
> It is better to go to the house of mourning
>> than to go to the house of feasting,
> for this is the end of all mankind,
>> and the living will lay it to heart.
> Sorrow is better than laughter,
>> for by sadness of face the heart is made glad.
> The heart of the wise is in the house of mourning,
>> but the heart of fools is in the house of mirth. (ESV)

What is the Teacher teaching us here? That there is a kind of clarity to the reality of the human situation. Death is serious, we fall short of glory, and suffering is a kind of intrusion of reality into the midst of careless and thoughtless living.

While I was reading through Ecclesiastes with one dying friend, another friend of mine died of a brain tumor, and I was called to preach her funeral. I preached Ecclesiastes 7:2—"It is better to go to the house of mourning." Why?

So much of what we angle for in terms of ministry success is a kind of fine perfume. It's luxurious. It's valuable. It smells good. But even better is a "good name," an identity that holds fast when the scent wears off. The day of birth, the day of smelling good, and the day of feasting are all good things. But you find out who you are in the days of death. It's clarifying to suffer these little deaths in ministry *because you find out what you're in it for.* You find out if you're really a pastor, actually, or just a guy who wants to be applauded.

And hostility clarifies where others stand, what *they're* in it for, as well. My two biggest critics in my ministry started out as two of my biggest fans. The hostility became clarifying about where their true interests were, what they were really about. Hostility is clarifying.

## Hostility Is Normal

What the book of Ecclesiastes does for us is normalize lament. The book is a normalization of confusion, of weakness, of grief-stricken bewilderment. If you feel lost, hopeless, helpless, or overwhelmed, the Teacher is saying, "You're normal." Now, this isn't how God designed the world to work. It's not "normal" in the sense that he originally made the world good and mankind without sin. But, given the fallenness that ensued, the sin in the heart of every man, woman, and child, and the sheer relational dysfunction and cultural brokenness of the world, hostility is normal. We should be surprised when it *doesn't* happen.

If we're going to do relationships in this broken world, we're going to face conflict. If we're going to do relationships in the context of the church—a place where strangers don't just become friends, but enemies become brothers and sisters, where the Devil wants to disrupt the entire enterprise—we're going to have to go into that house of mourning time and time again. We need to lay this to heart: the normal course of ministry is fraught with conflict. That's totally normal.

But even if you've got huge problems in your church, potential splits or division, know that's not God's design for the church, but in this sinful world, it's normal. You're not unique. You're not special. Nobody's picking on you. You didn't end up in the one church in the world where incredibly awful things are said or done. You ended up in the crosshairs of the gospel and, subsequently, in the crosshairs of Satan. Just read the New Testament if you think hostility is out of the ordinary for the ministry of the church.

Don't say, "Why were the former days better than these?" (Eccl 7:10 ESV), since it is not wise of you to ask this. Wisdom comes in knowing hostility is normal. In fact, hostility is *due* the minister of the gospel. If you preach the gospel, you *will* stir some things up. The same sun that melts the ice hardens the clay. The Good Shepherd promises: "In the world you will have tribulation" (John

16:33 ESV). The pastor to whom the Lord entrusted his flock says, "Beloved, do not be surprised at the fiery trial when it comes upon you to test you, as though something strange were happening to you" (1 Peter 4:12 ESV).

Don't let hostility push you into self-pity. Don't let it push you into bitterness. Peter continues, "But rejoice insofar as you share Christ's sufferings, that you may also rejoice and be glad when his glory is revealed" (4:13 ESV).

## Hostility Pushes Us to God

Hostility draws us nearer to the God of peace. Or it can. It should.

The closer to God we get, the more wisdom we attain, wisdom that goes beyond ministerial technology, best practices, and pastoral strategies. We get real knowledge of God, which leads to real godliness, which is wisdom—treasure in the midst of poverty.

The Teacher writes in Ecclesiastes 7:8–12,

> Better is the end of a thing than its beginning,
>> and the patient in spirit is better than the proud in spirit.
> Be not quick in your spirit to become angry,
>> for anger lodges in the heart of fools.
> Say not, "Why were the former days better than these?"
>> For it is not from wisdom that you ask this.
> Wisdom is good with an inheritance,
>> an advantage to those who see the sun.
> For the protection of wisdom is like the protection of money,
>> and the advantage of knowledge is that wisdom preserves
>>> the life of him who has it. (ESV)

Character, pastor, is better than success. And wisdom is better than know-how. What does this wisdom look like?

Well, it looks first like learning the compassion our Shepherd has for others who have suffered in the same ways. You will serve people better through your wounds. The suffering of hostility makes you a better pastor to those who have been hurt. It's hard to shepherd biblically with a swagger. But with a limp? You become a blessing to the sheep in ways you and they never imagined.

The wisdom that comes from the experience of hostility also helps you discern the difference between the patient spirit (v. 8) and the rush to anger (v. 9). How do you know when to stick up for yourself, and how do you know when to suffer conflict without defense?

In 1 Corinthians 6:7, Paul says to the church embroiled in retribution against one another, "Why not rather be wronged?" But elsewhere he confronts Peter to his face. He names the names of divisive people. He calls the Galatians foolish. When hostility pushes us to God, it ushers us into the wisdom of knowing when we're only seeking personal retribution or if the gospel and the safety of the flock are at stake. Wisdom is knowing the difference. Is the conflict simply something at which you've taken offense? An interpersonal difference? Or does it compromise the gospel, the mission, and the integrity of the church?

Sometimes protecting someone from the church, or the church from someone, puts us in the position of taking the heat. And this is, in God's long-range plan for us, good. The potential of having our reputation tarnished, brothers, puts us in the position of Christ.

Philip Ryken, in his commentary on Ecclesiastes 7, particularly commenting on verses 2–3, says, "Dealing with death, in all its sorrow, makes us better people."[2] More than making us better people, however, it conforms us more to the image of the greatest Person, Jesus Christ. Hostility can push us into the likeness of Christ, for *he* was not above it. He suffered it. He was tempted in it.

Jesus knows what it's like to have those Pharisees in the foyer trying to trap him in his words. He knows what it's like to have those Sadducees in the sanctuary conspiring against him. He knows what

---

2. Philip Graham Ryken, *Ecclesiastes: Why Everything Matters* (Wheaton, IL: Crossway, 2010), 154.

it's like to have those foes in the fellowship hall jealous about his influence. He knows what it's like to have the crowd that cheered turn on a dime to jeer.

Jesus knows what it's like to have well-meaning coleaders object to his vision and misunderstand him. He knows what it's like to have friends who abandon him or who sleep while he agonizes. He knows what it's like to have passive fellow pastors willing to let him take all the hits while they watch from the safety of the shadows.

He was willing to be tempted as we are. He was willing to suffer. He endured more heat than you and I could ever or will ever take. Jesus walked straight into the hostility of the cross—for you.

Hostility is part of God's plan to make you more reliant on him and to make you more like Jesus. In that regard, hostility is normal in this broken world.

## Hostility Is Governed by God

The Teacher writes in Ecclesiastes 7:13–14,

> Consider the work of God:
> who can make straight what he has made crooked?

> In the day of prosperity be joyful, and in the day of adversity consider: God has made the one as well as the other, so that man may not find out anything that will be after him. (ESV)

Brother, the Lord made you for this. You can trust that Christ is not above your pain now, because he wasn't above it at the cross. If He stood in your place then, why would He not be standing by you now? He is indeed walking with you. He walked before you. He is above your circumstances now only in the sense that he is the sovereign Lord who governs it for your good. You can have all the confidence this knowledge affords. You might not have seen it coming, but he did. Nothing catches him off guard. You may not know what they're saying behind your back, but he hears it all, and he is handling it. His governance is for your good.

So, what do you do with this? You remind yourself—and if necessary, your church—that *you are not an employee.* You are a pastor. And the Lord, in his wisdom, has stewarded this situation to you. In his wisdom, he decided this difficulty was tailor-made for you, for your leadership, for your gifts, for your disposition, and for your responsibility. Not to prove your greatness, but to prove his.

"In the day of prosperity be joyful, and in the day of adversity consider: God has made the one as well as the other, so that man may not find out anything that will be after him" (Eccl. 7:14 ESV). You don't know what tomorrow holds. But you know he holds tomorrow. So, you can shepherd joyfully, compassionately, wisely, confidently, directly, and graciously. You can do all things through the one who strengthens you (Phil 4:13).

## Church Discipline

By God's grace, many kinds of personal conflicts within the church can be neutralized by parties willing to repent and forgive and be reconciled to each other. But some conflicts are more complex than personal disagreements. Sometimes in a sinner's lack of repentance there is *a lack* of conflict, an ambivalence about their sin and an unwillingness to crucify the flesh and fight for holiness. In these and other cases of unrepentant sin that threatens to harm the church or the witness of the church, we have outlined in Scripture guidance for the severe mercy of church discipline.

For some, church discipline will always be objectionable because it seems outdated and unnecessary. But for many, their objection is simply a reflection of not knowing what the Bible teaches on the matter. If a church never broaches the subject until its response to someone's unrepentant sin must be made public, church discipline will always seem alien. Statements will abound like, "What are you doing bringing all this law into a place that should be filled with grace?" We have to preach the relevant texts to our congregation. And we have to make both the privileges and the obligations of membership clear in our interviews of those joining the church.

One word of caution, however: Some churches love teaching the process of church discipline all out of proportion; they love it *too much*. In some church environments, church discipline is mainly equated with the nuclear option of excommunication and the leadership of the church is not known for its patience but, rather, for its itchy trigger finger. Teaching the process of church discipline is not about filling the church with a sense of dread and covering the floor with eggshells. It's about providing enough visibility about the guardrails and expectations that people can actually breathe more freely, not less. Church discipline—rightly exercised—is motivated by real, sorrowful love and concern.

Sometimes, the avoidance of discipline masquerades as love and concern. In seeking to avoid conflicts, the church has avoided the biblical mandate of church discipline, not realizing that it is hatred of God and the church not to practice it. "It is for discipline that you have to endure," the author of Hebrews writes. "God is treating you as sons. For what son is there whom his father does not discipline? If you are left without discipline, in which all have participated, then you are illegitimate children and not sons" (12:7–8 ESV). The Lord disciplines those he loves (Rev 3:19). And this is what church discipline is in its broadest sense—*a love-driven training of the church toward Christlikeness*. Discipline is training in godliness and it helps a church grow in love for God and obedience to his commands.

For this reason, we see that discipline doesn't begin when someone must be excommunicated from a church. It begins long before and is seeking to avoid that end. It begins with the regular preaching of the gospel. This is a training of the church to cherish Christ and his work and to believe all the doctrine that emerges from it. But when someone demonstrates *professed* disbelief, whether in espousing heterodoxy or in a pattern of sin, the church has a recourse for addressing this in ways that aim to restore truth and peace.

"If your brother or sister sins," Jesus commands, "go and point out their fault, just between the two of you. If they listen to you, you have won them over" (Matt 18:15). Notice the burden is on the offended party. Why? I think it is because, very often, offenders can be ignorant of their offense (and thus unrepentant). But it's also because the offended party—whether elders acting on behalf of the church or another brother or sister who's been sinned against—is making it clear that they desire restoration of fellowship, that they want reconciliation. This pictures the forgiveness of God, in which the Son comes seeking *us*.

Jesus says to make this initial meeting peaceful (the intention is to "win" the brother or sister, not conquer them) and private ("between the two of you"). These are the only two options in interpersonal conflict. If someone has hurt us, intentionally or not, our only two biblical options are to either take up the matter with them in the interest of reconciliation or to let it go, forgiving them in our hearts. Bitter unforgiveness is not an option. Tearing them down to anyone who will listen is not an option. In many instances, sins committed against us require us to fight against our need for vengeance and fight for the desire to make peace. "If they listen to you, you have won them over." And this was the goal all along: not a fight, but peace—a dwelling together in unity.

What is pictured in the beginning of the process is an informal (but intentional) encounter. Many times, the potential trouble can be nipped in the bud. But sometimes it isn't: "But if they will not listen, take one or two others along, so that 'every matter may be established by the testimony of two or three witnesses'" (Matt 18:16). When someone is confronted about their sin or false belief, however peaceably, often an internal defense lawyer emerges. The lawyer helps them negotiate a peace without repentance. They spin, dismiss, or ignore. Sometimes they argue. Thus, Jesus commands an external adjudication. The sphere of confrontation is slightly expanded to include "one or two others." Now it's getting more serious.

Still, the aim is peace. So, what do the witnesses do? They observe the conversation between the offended and alleged offender. They try to remain impartial. They consult the Word of God and pray. And they help render a verdict. Weighing the evidence, they say either to the offended, "You are wrong about your charge, and you should let this go," or to the offender, "You have sinned against your brother or sister, and you should repent." It should be put more gently than that, of course, but not indistinctly so.

If found in the wrong, perhaps the offender will now repent given the weight of others confirming his sin. This process may take some time. It should not be rushed, but neither should it be left to languish. We are trusting the Holy Spirit, who is allegedly in residence in our brother or sister to convict them and also empower them to repent and ask for forgiveness. We will express all of this with love.

But unrepentance is ugly. "If they still refuse to listen, tell it to the church; and if they refuse to listen even to the church, treat them as you would a pagan or a tax collector" (Matt 18:17). We've now reached the penultimate level of seriousness. It's still possible the offender has a legitimate plea of innocence. Maybe the offended and the witnesses *have* gotten it all wrong. Who must adjudicate now? The church, as led by the pastors.

At this point, we must make sure the sin really is a pattern of sin that promises to bring reproach upon the church body. We must make sure the offender really is unrepentantly disinterested in aligning him-or herself with the pattern of sound teaching or godly living to which they have previously committed. Nothing about any of this end of the process should be vague or based on feelings.

At each stage of the process, the goal is not punishment but peace, not revenge but reconciliation. This last phase may take the most time. Patient elders will plead, pray, and urge. There may be righteous anger involved, but more so, there is heartbroken sadness.

It is a spiritually dangerous position for an offender to "refuse to listen even to the church." But we must be clear about what constitutes being "in" the church so that we know how and when to put someone "out" of it. A failure to do this may feel gracious and tolerant, but it is a way of saying that bodily health and witness mean nothing.

The godly response to a stubbornly unrepentant member is to "treat them as you would a pagan or a tax collector." Jesus is saying to treat the unrepentant like they're unbelievers. The church essentially ratifies what the offender has chosen with their unrepentance. The offender, at this point, will be removed from church membership and asked not to partake of the Lord's Supper. They may or may not be asked to withdraw from the gathering of the church, depending on the nature of the unrepentance. In most circumstances, excommunicated members do not wish to attend worship anyway, but sometimes they do.

The picture in Matthew 18 is of a personal conflict that has grown to affect the whole body. In 1 Corinthians 5, Paul addresses the sort of disobedience that is immediately public. This might include publicly false teaching or publicly known sexual immorality. The church discipline process is rather abrupt and formal from the beginning:

> I wrote to you in my letter not to associate with sexually immoral people—not at all meaning the sexually immoral of this world, or the greedy and swindlers, or idolaters, since then you would need to go out of the world. But now I am writing to you not to associate with anyone who bears the name of brother if he is guilty of sexual immorality or greed, or is an idolater, reviler, drunkard, or swindler—not even to eat with such a one. For what have I to do

with judging outsiders? Is it not those inside the church whom you are to judge? God judges those outside. "Purge the evil person from among you." (1 Cor 5:9–13 ESV)

Here is a formal shunning meant to protect the body and snap the offender to attention, as elsewhere Paul writes, "I urge you, brothers and sisters, to watch out for those who cause divisions and put obstacles in your way that are contrary to the teaching you have learned. Keep away from them" (Rom 16:17). And then later, "Take special note of anyone who does not obey our instruction in this letter. Do not associate with them, in order that they may feel ashamed. Yet do not regard them as an enemy, but warn them as you would a fellow believer" (2 Thess 3:14–15).

These instances seem to involve gross public sin that is instantly known and clearly taints the church's witness. The most notable example of such a sin today is likely the sexual abuse of children. For the safety of the most vulnerable of your lambs, such a proven offender should be removed from the flock, whether they profess repentance or not. This does justice to the body by doing justice for the victim. Victims should be the chief concern in this moment.

If such an offender is, indeed, repentant, they will submit to proper authorities and accept whatever consequences are due them. And if free to attend worship, they can do so somewhere else, having alerted that leadership of their sin and intention to be held accountable for it. People disinterested in Christ and his church and growing in the faith can't agree to any of this accountability, of course. Or, if they do, it will be found out.

Jesus closes his instructions for church discipline with a startling assurance: "Truly, I say to you, whatever you bind on earth shall be bound in heaven, and whatever you loose on earth shall be loosed in heaven" (Matt 18:18 ESV). D. A. Carson writes: "The church of Jesus the Christ is more than an audience. It is a group with confessional standards. . . . The continuity of the church depends as much on discipline as on truth. Indeed, faithful promulgation of the latter both entails and presupposes the former.[3]

If you find all of this judgmental, as indeed some of your people undoubtedly will, note that we have been given this mystery to steward as well. We have been given the keys to the kingdom. What we do in the church is meant to reflect the goodness and righteousness of heaven. Christ gives us the very authority to feed the sheep and also to protect them. This is what church discipline is all about.

## Making Peace

The gospel is a word of peace (Eph 2:14–17). Therefore, the gospel-driven pastor is constantly seeking to cultivate God's peace within the congregation. Remember the prophetic call of Isaiah:

> Comfort, comfort my people, says your God.
> Speak tenderly to Jerusalem,
>     and cry to her
> that her warfare is ended . . . (40:1–2 ESV)

What is this if not a word of peace?

But sometimes we seek the wrong kind of peace, the kind that comes at any cost. We seek the illusion of peace at the cost of truth, of godliness, of doctrinal and spiritual unity. This is no peace at all. We heal the wounds of our people lightly to maintain the appearance of peace (Jer 6:14). This is the work of an unfaithful shepherd, the shepherd interested in saving his own skin and covering his own back. This is the work of hired hands.

I still remember the worst members' meeting I've ever experienced. I was accused explicitly and implicitly of all manner of things by a few disgruntled members. None of it was true. And I had

3. D. A. Carson, *Matthew: Chapters 13 through 28*, The Expositor's Bible Commentary (Grand Rapids: Zondervan, 1995), 374.

become used to simply "taking it." Before that meeting I had talked with my fellow elders about one sticky situation we were pastoring through, a potential church discipline issue. We knew the chance of being accused in our meeting with the involved parties was very high, and we agreed together that defending ourselves would not serve our desired ends. "Why not rather be wronged?" Paul says (1 Cor 6:7). That meeting was miserable, as I took the brunt of the complaints. I didn't defend myself. Neither did my fellow elders defend me. We had agreed on the illusion of peace.

This was my customary tack with complaints and criticisms. I would listen, consider, ask questions. I wouldn't admit fault where I could not in good conscience do so, but I typically found some way to apologize and ask for an opportunity to be better. I was defenseless to a fault. And in that members' meeting, I felt like a piñata. I sat in a pew with my back turned to the barrage of criticisms. And then I'd had enough. I had endured months of gossip and grumbling, weeks of lame complaints, and now an ungodly meeting full of accusations.

For the very first time in my pastorate, I publicly defended myself. I stood up and said something like, "I've heard a number of you say that people are hurt. But do you know who else is hurt? My wife and I are hurt. You have hurt us. And I should have said something before. But I'm saying it now." I calmly set down the microphone and walked out.

Later I felt terrible. I wrestled with whether I'd done the right thing. Maybe I should have done what I'd always done and just absorb the pain. That afternoon I talked to an older pastor friend of mine and relayed the story. To my embarrassment, he said, "Oh, Jared, you shouldn't have done that." That hurt me and sent me further within my heart. I began to discover that my pursuit of comfort up until that moment wasn't really a pursuit of peace. But neither was my "finally standing up for myself."

I'm still not sold that my defense was wrong. I see Paul speaking quite bluntly and regularly about the pain others caused him. But, in retrospect, I do know that my heart in that moment was not tuned to my own hopes in sanctification. I wasn't walking by the Spirit. I was just tired of reaping the bad fruit of my poor peacemaking up to that moment.

When we are sinfully accosted or maligned, it's not wrong to appropriately defend ourselves, especially since it's the shepherd's job to rebuke sin, even sin against himself. (Better yet, the unsung beauty of plurality is our brother-elders defending us, provided they aren't too scared to do it.) That's good and right and proper. And yet, we have to want something more than winning. In that moment, I was just fed up. But I wasn't thinking at all about feeding others— meaning, I had myself first in my heart, not my flock. You can't make peace if you're only interested in winning.

I am cut to the quick when I think of Jesus, while being murdered, crying out, "Father, forgive them, for they know not what they do" (Luke 23:34 ESV). And pastors, every day, as you mess all this up in a million little ways and a few big ones, Christ the Good Pastor is still our advocate and intercessor. His once-for-all sacrifice of blood covers the duration of your messy ministry—"Father, forgive him. He just doesn't know what he's doing." Thank God that Jesus's heart desires, above all, your sanctification. Thank God that the Good Shepherd's aim is that you would look like him.

At the end of that pastorate, one of my chief critics—one who had caused much emotional harm to me and my wife despite my appeals with them to understand and sort out the grievance—approached me to send me off to my next ministry assignment. "I just want you to know I wish you well." I looked up and said, "I don't believe you." I could not affirm the lie. I could not entertain the charade. It would not have been right for me or for them.

We cannot declare peace where there is none. We can't pretend our way to peace. Peace in the church is the result of the truth mutually affirmed. This means, above all, dealing with things as they actually are. Just as Christ only deals with us on the playing field of reality, pastors should take care not to interact with what they think people mean or what they think was said, but with the actual facts of the matter. This will involve uncomfortable, potentially conflict-ripe situations, but truth-telling that leads to resolution is far better than stewing in solitude or, perhaps even worse, gossiping and grumbling with your perceived allies.

Different situations may call for different approaches, but the direct approach is almost always best. Proverbs 4:24 tells us to avoid "crooked speech" (ESV), by which we may interpret it to mean avoiding dishonesty but also talk about others that is circuitous around them. It is the opposite of straight talk. Some may find the direct approach to making peace puzzling, as it sometimes leads us directly into conflict! But very often true peace is found through difficult, perhaps even tense, conversations. The peace found in the avoidance of necessary conversations or confrontations is a false peace.

The pastor will likely find himself subject to passive-aggressive criticism or anonymous complaints. In such cases, it is important to clear the air. If there is something of merit in the complaint, own what you can. Apologize and repent, if necessary. But in any event, the best approach to gossip or sinful criticism is to head it off at the pass.

The Lord does not call pastors to a martyr's complex. Taking the kind of hypothetical high road that would subject yourself to becoming someone's doormat neither benefits you *nor them*. It is not good pastoral practice to let congregants conduct sinful speech or divisive talk, and this includes when these are aimed at you. The goal of all human relationships, in alignment with the gospel, is the magnifying of Christ and the unity he imparts between sinners and himself and between sinners and other sinners, "that they may all be one" (John 17:21 ESV).

I remember the day I realized a dear lady in my congregation had been recently cold toward me. It was distressing because we'd previously enjoyed a very friendly relationship. She was an older saint who had been through some very difficult things in her life—an unbelieving husband who cheated on her and abandoned her, an unbelieving son who was in bondage to drug addiction—and I had counseled her through much suffering. Then one day I realized she was more aloof, not as talkative with me as she'd been before.

My tendency is to let such things play out. That, I assumed, would be the easiest thing to do. After all, if she had a problem with me, she should bear the responsibility of bringing it up. Right? I considered the words of Christ in Matthew 5:23. If you realize your brother or sister has something against *you*, it is imperative to seek reconciliation. This put the responsibility on me. As a Christian, I must bear it. As a pastor, I must bear it.

So I went directly to her, asking if I'd offended or hurt her in some way. She was grateful for my approach because, indeed, she had been hurt by me in a conversation weeks prior. It turned out to be a misunderstanding. She had misheard something I'd said and thus misinterpreted my response to something she was telling me. We were reconciled. But imagine if I'd just let it go. The absence of conflict would not have been the presence of peace.

Thus, with both intentionally divisive people and with innocently offended people, the best course of action is the direct one. Ask questions. Humbly listen. Seek peace directly. You will learn to discern this wisdom day to day, in situations great and small. Sometimes it takes fighting and sometimes it takes surrendering, but we must give to our flocks what Christ has given us: "Peace I leave with you; my peace I give you" (John 14:27).

## For Reflection

1. Is it your tendency to rush into conflict or to avoid it? Why do you think that is?
2. How can you discern the difference between protecting a

church from one person and protecting one person from the church?

3. How do you know the difference between a valid criticism and someone who is critically divisive?

4. Why do you think too few churches today still neglect to practice biblical church discipline?

5. What are some ways the gospel informs a pastor's approach to conflict and peace in a church?

## For Further Study:

Bonhoeffer, Dietrich. *Life Together: A Discussion of Christian Fellowship.* New York: Harper & Row, 1954.

Outside the Scriptures, no book has been more formative in my own thinking and feeling about the church. There is no better book on how the gospel of grace ought to shape and sustain the experience of Christian community.

Powlison, David. *Safe and Sound: Standing Firm in Spiritual Battles.* Greensboro, NC: New Growth, 2019.

What begins as an enlightening survey of the nature of spiritual warfare (through Ephesians 6) eventually becomes a reliable guide to counseling others through the various kinds of conflicts and afflictions faced by Christians.

Schaeffer, Francis A. *True Spirituality: How to Live for Jesus Moment by Moment.* 30th anniversary ed. Carol Stream, IL: Tyndale House, 2001.

Perhaps the spiritual heir of Bonhoeffer as it pertains to Christian spirituality in the life of the church, Schaeffer situates the experience of fruitful relationship with Christ in its proper context of fruitful relationships within the church. His chapter on healing in personal relationships is especially pertinent for the navigation and resolution of conflict.

CHAPTER 9

# LIVING

It is midweek, but Sunday is coming. Your desk is arrayed with commentaries and other reference texts. You have pen and paper, laptop and Logos, and your Bible is under your nose. The text is calling to you, taming you, mastering you. You toil away by lamplight.

Over the next several days, even as you run errands, carry out administrative tasks, play with your kids, and meet with church folks, the sermon is brewing in your brain. Your mind and your heart are mulling it, chewing it, and gnawing on the text like a dog with a bone.

You pray over your sermon, you stare at your outline until the structure seems to sing, and come Saturday night, you're still at the kitchen table, pen between your teeth, your brow furrowed, and your eyes on the prize. If you could sweat blood over this word, you would. Your wife brings you a cup of coffee, puts her hand on your shoulder. She says, "Our church is so lucky to have you." You look up at her, beaming, and say, "I know."

You can hardly sleep Saturday night. You wake up before the alarm goes off. You'd been preaching in your sleep. You are preaching in the shower. You are preaching in the car on the drive over.

You are rarin' to go. This is it! This is the day the Lord has made. It is time once again to part the waters. You are shaking hands, pinching the cheeks of babies.

During the worship in song, you feel as though you could fly away. Your hands are raised, your heart begins to beat more quickly, there is a good knot in your stomach, and you practically bound up to the pulpit when it's time to deliver the sermon.

It is so good. It is the best biblical oratory delivered in at least a five-mile radius and at least since the Sunday before. Your exposition is meaty. Your illustrations are stirring. Your application is convicting. The turns of phrases are clever, the insights are deep, and the proclamations are strong. You could *die* in that pulpit.

You look out to the eager faces before you, the woolly sheep who have gathered into the pen this morning to be fed wisdom from on high. You see more than a few faces lit up—but not with wonder. With the electronic glow of their illuminated phones. "I hope they're on their Bible app," you think to yourself. A few people look angry. A few people are definitely asleep. A few laugh, but not when you told a joke. Many are smiling, you are glad to see, but their eyes do not seem to register what you are saying. Their smiles, you fear, are the smiles of Sunday morning routines, a kind of grin-and-bear-it grimace.

When you pronounce the words, "In conclusion," they seem a little too responsive. You hear a symphony of Bibles being slapped shut across the room. People sit up straight, anticipating standing for the last song and rushing to pick up the kiddos. You are done and you pray. They fold up their message notes in their bulletin outlines and stick them in their Bibles. They put them in their back pockets, where they will sit on them. You picture the outline you have worked up from the core of your being and the cellar of intellectual affliction being shoved down into the side pocket of car doors along with junk mail and wadded up McDonald's wrappers.

Then you go home. Your wife, oddly, says nothing. You get up on

Monday morning after hitting snooze three times. You head into the office and sit at your desk and look at your calendar and your email inbox and a blank page where next Sunday's sermon is supposed to begin, and you think, "What am I doing?"

In a world of religious noise, with so much competing for our attention, to what should we actually devote that attention? In a church culture that offers countless steps and tips and helpful hints, a million ways to pull ourselves up by our bootstraps, what is the biblical shepherd actually called to do? The spirits of pragmatism and consumerism so easily creep into our thinking—into our very modes of being—that we forget both how to be a pastor and how to be a human being.

## Abiding in Christ

Much of evangelicalism suffers because of pastors who have forgotten they are not cogs in a wheel, parts of a machine. The pastor becomes a disseminator of spiritual information or a kind of CEO or entrepreneur. But the pastor is not fundamentally an employee. He is the lead worshiper. As such, the pastor must live his life and conduct his ministry as a sacrifice of praise to God, which means, of course, that his personal spirituality and private religious practice must be devoted to the glory of God alone. In order to feed others, the shepherd must himself feed. In order to point others to Christ, the shepherd must be familiar with Christ and have a cultivated relationship with Christ.

I have covered the pastor as worshiper in chapter 3, but it is worth reiterating here that no pastor can honestly and effectively take others where he is not himself going. If it's all a ruse, just an exercise in religious role play, we will eventually crash and burn. And if we are constantly pouring out into our churches without drinking regularly from the living water ourselves, we will end up husks of men before it's all said and done. I don't need to rehearse the sobering statistics of fallen or otherwise neutralized leaders for this to hit home. If we're honest with ourselves, we feel it in our bones.

The first habit that we must adopt to ensure that we are well fed is to pray as if our lives depended upon it. I know this is the umpteenth time I've urged prayer in this book, but there is a reason for that. When the book is finished, I still will not have emphasized it enough. We need an honest and open dialogue with God. He speaks to us in his Word. You speak to him in prayer. How on earth do you expect to see a relationship sustained where there is no communication?

We have nothing to offer that does not come from God. And our health as a spiritual person is dependent on the grace of God. The very Lord of the Universe wants to hear from us. He wants to gather us up onto his lap each day and hear our concerns, our hurts, our fears, our joys, and our requests. This is such a shocking privilege, having the ear of the Almighty, that we ought always to feel convicted about our failure to avail ourselves of it. Sinner, we have access! We have access to the holy God who loves us despite us. He does not fold his arms and "tsk-tsk" about you.

We often don't pray because it doesn't feel immediately productive or efficient. And this is all the more reason we must give ourselves to prayer. We need our self-orientation squashed. We need our self-interest vanquished. When we pray, we submit to God's God-ness and our own creatureliness. So, *pray like your very life depends on it.* Because it does.

The flip side of this open communication is the second habit pastors must cling to for dear life: listening to God. He is speaking through his Word. We may believe he is speaking in other ways too, and I am fine with that myself, but the way he speaks objectively, authoritatively, inerrantly, infallibly, and sufficiently is through his Word. You really don't need any other word, because what we have in the Scriptures is enough to make us "complete, equipped for every good work" (2 Tim 3:17 ESV).

Pastor, we need a daily dwelling in Jesus. Don't, therefore, simply use the Word for your next sermon. Use it for your own filling, your own sustaining, your own living. *When we open that book, God is speaking to us.* Open the Bible, then, every day with reverence and expectancy and wonder. We are hearing from on high.

The spiritual disciplines are so necessary for abiding in Christ. But there are other practices that contribute to a pastor's healthy personhood and ministry, as well.

## Establishing Rhythms for Healthy Ministry

These practices are suggested to remind us of our dependence. They put us in tune with our finitude, our creatureliness. Driven by grace, these pastoral rhythms can help us stifle the temptation to justification by success or approval and put us back in a place of experiencing God's true power.

### Meditate on Your Qualifications

It's astounding to me how little awareness the general evangelical public shows of the biblical qualifications for eldership. There are standards given for pastors—pastors must be *this* tall to ride this ride—and we like to think, "It'll be fine. We'll hold on to him. Why should everybody else get to have fun?" And then, we're shocked when guys get thrown from the car when it rockets through a loop.

By way of reminder, here is 1 Timothy 3:2–7:

> Therefore an overseer must be above reproach, the husband of one wife, sober-minded, self-controlled, respectable, hospitable, able to teach, not a drunkard, not violent but gentle, not quarrelsome, not a lover of money. He must manage his own household well, with all dignity keeping his children submissive, for if someone does not know how to manage his own household, how will he care for God's church? He must not be a recent convert, or he may

become puffed up with conceit and fall into the condemnation of the devil. Moreover, he must be well thought of by outsiders, so that he may not fall into disgrace, into a snare of the devil. (ESV)

Taking this passage and its parallels in Titus 1 and 1 Peter 5 in composite, what do we see? An eagerness for ministry does not equate to a qualification. A sense of call does not equate to qualification. Skills and gifts do not authenticate qualification. The only skill set mentioned is "able to teach." The rest are character issues, spiritual dispositions, and personal qualities. It says nothing about dynamic leadership, vision casting, or being a catalytic anything. (Those aren't bad things, but they aren't qualifications.)

Do we ponder this high bar? Not in a legalistic, self-pitying way, but in a humble, self-evaluative way. We should, in fact, meditate on our qualifications more than our accomplishments. Our accomplishments adorn our qualifications, but they should never replace them.

What do we know of the high-profile ministerial collapses? Most of these men disqualified themselves long before they'd fallen. They began to coast, propelled by their reputations. They measured themselves (and instructed others to measure them) solely by their gifts and their successes. Sometimes we even see some fallen pastors angling for a quick comeback, saying that their disqualification *is* their qualification. This is a great way of thumbing one's nose at the Scriptures.

Take a long, hard look at the biblical qualifications and ask yourself how you're doing. Ponder Paul's list of the fruit of the Spirit in Galatians 5:22–23 and ask yourself how you're growing in those dispositions. Or better yet, ask your wife, a trusted colleague, or a friend to do it for you.

One of the most revealing exercises our married residents undertake in the Pastoral Training Center is interviewing their wives. Each married resident must ask his wife to rate his resemblance to each of the biblical qualifications for ministry and explain why she chose the rating she did. Who better to know if you are growing in gentleness or self-control than the one who knows you best?

You may ask how this rhythm could be considered gospel driven. It seems awfully judgy! But because these qualities are things developed by the Holy Spirit in us, by the power of grace in our lives, honest evaluation of ourselves is not just a way to gauge our deficiencies, but also to notice the ongoing work of Christ in our lives. The power of progressive sanctification is such that we may not be what we ought to be, but by the Spirit we are also not what we used to be!

## Fast from Being Needed

The religious dynamic in many churches where the pastor supplies the ministry and the people supply the need for the ministry creates a deformed kind of religious co-dependence. What often results from this dynamic is a presumptuous and idolatrous level of expectation on the pastor. We must shepherd wisely to keep our congregations from becoming co-dependent with us (or us with them). Are you addicted to being needed?

This addiction can be remedied through a strategic withholding of oneself—not a distancing, nor a neglect of real duty and care, nor an insulation or isolation. That is in direct violation of Peter's command to shepherd the flock among us (1 Peter 5:2) and Jesus's command to feed the sheep (John 21:17). But the pastor's role is to equip the saints for ministry (Eph 4:12), and this can't happen if he does all the ministry himself. It is good to regularly hold back enough that if you were to get hit by a bus today, your church can live (and grow!) without you. Very few churches advertise for a pastor who will lead a church in such a way that they don't need him very much, but wise pastors will work toward pushing their church's dependency onto Christ.

There are a variety of ways to resist the development of co-dependency, including:

- Establishing a plurality of elders or releasing into ministry the plurality of elders you already have. This assumes that these elders will be biblical elders and not church businessmen or trustees operating under an inaccurate title.
- Observing the Sabbath, taking your day(s) off, and using your vacation time. The people of the church will survive. I promise.
- Taking a sabbatical if you have reached the stage of qualifying for one.
- Sharing the preaching duties, not just when you're out of town.
- Getting serious about leadership development and replication.
- Putting your family's health above your church's expectations.
- Delegating.
- Not attending every church program or function.

Pastor, your church wants a Savior. You're not him. You are not Jesus, and you can't be available 24–7 like he can. This rhythm is gospel-driven because only in the confidence of the gospel can you relinquish the fear of man and the rush of being needed in order to rest. Fasting from being needed is a practice driven by grace, because only in the humility of the gospel can we embrace our creatureliness enough to enter rest.

## Commune with Jesus as an Actual Person

Too many pastors are gospel-centered in idea or paradigm but not in person. They have a relationship with *the idea* of Christ. They deny themselves the profound joy and extraordinary power in the simple privilege of knowing Christ and being his friend. I am thrilled by passages like Exodus 33:11, where we learn that "the LORD would speak to Moses face to face, as one speaks to a friend." Of course, we can't see him face to face, but we *will*. He has a face that can be seen. He has a voice that can be heard. He has arms that hug and hands that hold. Do you relate to Jesus daily under that reality?

My friend Ray Ortlund has taught me about this more than any other pastor I've known. When I walk away from an encounter with Ray, I feel as though I have encountered Jesus. He reminds me that Jesus is real, that Jesus can be known. How? Because I have the unmistakable impression that Ray *actually knows* Jesus, that he's actually friends with Jesus. And I have learned just from the sanctifying drudgery of ministry itself just how important it is for the shepherd of God's people *to be friends with God.*

This rhythm is gospel-driven because it is by belief in the gospel—by faith in Christ—that we are united to Christ, crucified with him, raised with him, seated with him in the heavenly places, and hidden with him in God. You have, by the gospel, not just a relationship with Christianity but a relationship *with Christ*, a communion with the living God.

## Return to the Gospel for Your Validation

Pastors too often find their confidence and justification in some vision of ministry success—the numeric growth of their church, the popularity of their ministry in the community, their spiritual feelings, etc. Pastors, we need to be tuned to a deeper reality, a foundation that holds sure through gain and loss, increase and decrease, victory and defeat. The reality is that the kingdom of God is unshakable. Faithfulness to its values and trust in its promises will ensure success both in season and out. This is good news, because it means God's approval of us is not based on our production.

When we ourselves cling to the gospel, it will shape us, giving us the mind and heart of Christ for our people. The grace of God is so clarifying for the pastor drunk on idols of success and ministerial performance. When we try to leverage the glory of Christ to get our own glory in the validation of people's approvals or accolades or the size of our congregations or platforms, the prophetic word cuts through the strange fire of our self-focused worship. Our grounding is not the ministry. Our grounding is the gospel.

This is, in fact, why Monday morning can be the most powerful moment in the shepherd's week. It can be the most powerful moment in the shepherd's week *because* it is the weakest. Because you stare at that blank page and that full inbox and you think, "What am I doing?" And the Spirit of the Lord prefers this. He prefers the weakness so that the strength of God can be magnified (2 Cor 12:9). He prefers the emptiness so that the fullness of grace can be exalted. He prefers the open hand of faith so that Christ will be our justification. Remember, pastors, it is not the strength of the faith that justifies but the strength of the Savior. And there is no stronger savior than the Lord Jesus Christ, who has all strength. The gospel is our validation, even in our weakness.

It is notable that Peter, in his reminder and application of the qualifications for ministry, does not hold out ecclesial success as the fruit of the faithful ministry. No. Instead he says, "shepherd the flock of God that is among you. . . . And when the chief Shepherd appears, you will receive the unfading crown of glory" (1 Peter 5:2, 4 ESV). And then he does it again, issuing another short round of exhortations and following it with this promise: "And after you have suffered a little while, the God of all grace, who has called you to his eternal glory in Christ, will himself restore, confirm, strengthen, and establish you" (5:10 ESV). Peter continually points pastors to their true confidence, their heavenly grounding, and their ultimate justification—Christ and his grace.

If you want to experience power and peace in your ministry, add these rhythms to your worshipful pursuit of the spiritual disciplines.

Spiritual rhythms are necessary for healthy discipleship and, thus, healthy pastoring. But in seeking longevity in a healthy ministry, there are also some physical rhythms discussed below that complement the spiritual quite effectively.

# Avoiding Burnout

Most faithful ministry leaders I know are tired. Many are the good kind of tired—they work hard, stay diligent and productive, and love their churches and ministries well. But many are the bad kind of tired—they overwork, they overcommit, and they're one or two more ministry crises or conflicts away from falling apart. So how can a pastor work to protect himself from crashing and burning?

He can incorporate the necessary ministry rhythm of RBM: *Rest. Boundaries. Margin.* Every pastor needs to intentionally and strategically make sure his ministry life includes the right amount of RBM.

## Rest

Rest is not optional. It's not a suggestion. God commanded it. Not every now and then—at least weekly. Every human being needs regular rest from work. A lot of pastors I know do not take a day off, or they spend their day "off" working on their sermon or doing other things that aren't exactly restful. You might say that your season of life does not allow for much rest, and I would say that you're setting yourself up for a disastrous next season.

## Boundaries

When I was pastoring, I committed Fridays to my wife. That was our day together. Once this became known, a couple of people in the church took it upon themselves to test this boundary, repeatedly asking for meetings on that day. But I protected it. Your boundaries might be different, but you still need them. I'm not talking about ignoring actual crisis or emergency situations. I'm just talking about regular ministry life.

It may sound noble and godly to keep convenience store hours, but it's a fast track to physical exhaustion and gradual resentment of the flock. A pastor without boundaries has an idolatry problem, and he is encouraging his church to have idolatry problems, too.

Repent of trying to be your church's functional messiah. Only Christ is omnipresent. Only Christ is omnipotent.

## Margin

Margin is similar to rest, but it's not about not working but about intentionally incorporating into your schedule open spaces for the quieter kind of work. Making sure I had plenty of margin in my ministry week for praying, reading, studying, and just *thinking* was extremely helpful. It's also a good preparation for the weeks when ministry burdens are unexpectedly heavy, or when there are surprise crisis situations or sudden counseling sessions needed.

If you've already scheduled your week to the limit with meetings and other ministry tasks, dealing with the occasional crises or surprises that come up will prevent you from completing necessary tasks, add burdens to support staff or other team members, overload your mental and emotional circuits, create a more frenetic week than necessary, and nullify your rest time. Incorporating margin allows you to be flexible and adaptive to the different needs of your ministry week to week. Schedule a reasonable amount of time of "free space" in your work week and use it in helpful, productive ways on things that could be set aside in the moment if something comes up.

It's not rocket science. Mind your RBM and you will go a good way toward protecting yourself from ministry burnout.

These disciplines aren't just a great gift to yourself, of course; they are a great gift to your family. Taking care to preserve your energy and thus your endurance has positive impacts on your mental and emotional health and the general well-being of your family, as you will have more time and energy to give to them and to love them well.

## Pastoring Your Family

One question I receive a lot from younger pastors or newly married pastors is this: "How do I know what to share with my wife?" The answer is largely a matter of discernment. The fact that you are "one flesh" (Gen 2:24) with your wife means that you will share with her the most difficult aspects of your life and ministry. This is part of what being married means—carrying one another's burdens, knowing each other thoroughly, and loving each other graciously. It is difficult to carry that out if there is no communication about what matters most.

And yet, the husband's role in the marriage is to "sanctify her, having cleansed her by the washing of water with the word" (Eph 5:26 ESV). Of course, it is the role of the Holy Spirit to conform any believer to the image of Christ (2 Cor 3:18). No husband, no matter how great, can manage that. But Paul appears to suggest in Ephesians that the husband's care for and edification of his wife in the faith is a kind of mirror to that work. Our aim, in other words, is our wives' purity and safety and glory.

This means that we must ensure that what we share of our troubles at church—and *how* we share what we share—is not leading our wives into temptation to bitterness, anger, or anxiety. I do not simply want to "unload" my burdens on my wife as a means of personal catharsis. I also do not want to share all my complaints and concerns and tempt her to join me in accusing the church or piling up grievances against it.

It is not wise to share "every little thing," even if the things are not necessarily little. Your wife probably doesn't need to know the rundown of your counseling information. But your wife likely does want to feel as if she's on your side, as if you're a team in this thing called marriage. She does not pastor the church with you, but she wants to feel she is *with you* as you pastor the church. This means first and foremost pastoring *her*.

"Husbands," Peter writes, "live with your wives in an understanding way, showing honor to the woman as the weaker vessel, since they are heirs with you of the grace of life, so that your prayers may not be hindered" (1 Peter 3:7 ESV). I take this command to understand and honor to mean, in part, that I am to be a good student of my wife. A pastoral husband will study his wife, not in a cold and distanced way, but as an interested lover. He will keep the lines of communication open, asking good, heart-level questions. He will ask for forgiveness often. He will ask for insight and advice. He will treat his wife like a glorious reflection of God, made in his image and uniquely wired for knowledge and intuition that he himself does not possess.

The pastor should put his wife first. He is not, after all, "one flesh" with the church. That is the role of Christ. It is certainly possible that some pastors sacrifice their churches on the altar of family, but far more often the reverse is true. Remember that you can always get another church, if it comes to that. You cannot (or should not!) get another wife. Embedded in the qualification "husband of one wife" (1 Tim 3:2 ESV) is a passionate commitment to the one with whom we are in covenant. She is our chief concern. She is our chief compassion. She is our chief love.

The apostle goes on to speak to pastors who are fathers: "He must manage his own household well, with all dignity keeping his children submissive" (1 Tim 3:4 ESV); and "his children are believers and not open to the charge of debauchery or insubordination" (Titus 1:6 ESV).

I remember the day I saw my teenage daughter reading a copy of *The Pastor's Kid* by Barnabas Piper. A bit of worry rose up in my heart. I did not grow up in a ministry family, but I was extra conscious of the reality of the "fishbowl" for pastor's families. My wife and I were intentional about never explicitly putting pressure on our daughters to act a certain way or speak a certain way *because they were pastor's kids.* I never wanted them to feel as though they had to perform for me or represent me. I asked my daughter, "Did you ever feel like we pressured you to live up to a certain standard because of what I do for a living?"

She said, "No, Dad, you guys never did that. But you didn't need to. The pressure was always there anyway." She went on to describe how simply being the pastor's kid made it difficult at school but especially in church. Sunday school teachers would say things like, "Oh, you probably know this material already." Church folks would make assumptions about my daughters' interests or knowledge or aptitude. This made them feel very self-conscious but also very bad when either they didn't know the answers to certain questions or they felt like they were embarrassing or dishonoring their parents for not representing us well.

Be aware of this pressure for your children, pastors. Yes, discipline them in the Lord. Raise them up to know the Scriptures and to be contributing members of the church family. But make it a point to say to them directly and often, "You are not your position in this family. You are not your Bible knowledge. Your approval is not based on your performance. You don't have to be my representative to the congregation. You only need to love Jesus and let me know how I can help you do that more."

And then really do that, brothers. Really do pursue your children's joy in the Lord above good grades, above good jobs, above looking religious, and above keeping up appearances. Pray for your kids daily and serve their affections for Christ.

## Pastoring as a Single Man

I do not take the qualifications about the pastor's marriage to mean that all pastors must be married. That Christ was not married is a worthy example. And while it is obviously an argument from silence, it would appear that a number of the apostles and early church leaders were single.

If you are a single pastor desirous of marriage, let me encourage you in the grace of God not to see marriage as the solution to all of your problems, whether loneliness or others. The absence of what we desire has a great tendency to make an idol of it.

Make no mistake, however, that if you desire marriage, you desire a good thing. There is no shame in that pursuit. But there can be shame in the way it is pursued. It is likely not a good idea to date from within your congregation. Aside from the natural power dynamics involved in such a relationship, there is the great potential for awkwardness and hurt feelings if the relationship does not work out. I would also caution single pastors against letting the desire for a wife consume his thoughts and distract him from his ministerial duties.

To the pastor who is committed to singleness, even if just for the time being, I want to encourage you to find your sufficiency in Christ. Do not let others shame you or ridicule you for your commitment to the church. But remember not to let your ministry become your identity. Do not let the church become your wife.

Consider the words of Paul: "To the unmarried and the widows I say that it is good for them to remain single, as I am" (1 Cor 7:8 ESV). Think of the advantages for ministry this season of life affords you. You are free to focus fully on the Lord's concerns and to pour in wholeheartedly to your church. To the best of your ability, think of your singleness not as a hindrance but as an advantage. Single pastors, there is nothing wrong with you. You are not less than. It is in fact "good" to remain single according to the word of the Lord.

## Building Friendships

It is extremely difficult for pastors to maintain healthy and close friendships, especially with those inside the church. There are a multitude of reasons for this. Sometimes it is the result of overworked pastors and their inability (or unwillingness) to treat the church as something more than a jobsite or project. But, many times, it is a result of the unspoken dynamic of congregational life. The pastor feels he must maintain a certain image or always be "on" to sustain his position or credibility. Whatever the reason, many pastors have few friends.

Be proactive about this. It sometimes takes years to be at ease enough in a congregation to be yourself in a safe way with other men in your church. But you can begin now sowing the seeds of friendship both within the church and without.

Seek out pastoral peers for coffee or lunches. Schedule times to hang out and fellowship. Go out on double dates. Do not see other pastors as competition but as a potential fraternity. Inside your congregation, schedule meetings that have nothing to do with your ministry agenda or projects. Just *be* with people.

The epidemic of loneliness is hitting middle-aged men especially hard. Some reckon the health impacts rival even those of obesity. It is possible that the younger generation may be correcting this trend, but the rise of consumerism in our culture and the inward turning of individualized technology are hard compulsions against community. Thus, every pastor should be on guard against his tendency to isolate or insulate.

## Being a Good Citizen

Part of living as a Christian is living as a witness to the reality of God in the world. This is highlighted among the requirements for pastors: "He must be well thought of by outsiders" (1 Tim 3:7 ESV). There are numerous ways to go about this, but ministers of the gospel ought to take great care to cultivate this qualification. Here are some important ways to achieve this end:

### Be Involved in Your Community

Do you have a third place where you can be a regular? The coffee shop, the café, the corner store, the gym, etc.? Be active, be present, and be friendly. Similarly, if your children are in school, be an active parent. Volunteer to chaperone field trips or to work lunchroom duties. Participate in school sports or on the school board. Are there other ways to "get out" and be a regular presence? Take advantage of those.

Becoming a regular at a third place and in your community is a great way to stay tuned in to the concerns and values of lost people. In addition to helping you get to know your community and its needs, it's also a vital way to build bridges for evangelistic engagement.

## Evangelize

Make a commitment to seek and seize opportunities to share the gospel with others. In order to do this, of course, you will not just need to exist outside your home and office but also engage with people outside those walls. Listen well and ask good questions. Try to connect. Look for openings to witness for Christ. Ask people if you can pray for them. You will find that as a pastor, religious conversations are very easy to get into. They simply arise from the normal chitchat with outsiders because of your vocation.

## Be Charitable

Are you known as a miser when the fundraisers come around? Will you refuse to buy Girl Scout cookies or patronize the neighborhood lemonade stand? Do you complain about poor service at restaurants? Are you the guy at the town hall meetings shouting down other leaders? Is your posture toward the community—or your church's posture toward the same—seen as antagonistic? There may be valid causes to fight for and injustices to correct, but can you do this graciously?

## Be Circumspect Online

The world is watching. If you are the pastor constantly arguing or posting angry political rants on social media, you are bearing witness to your true hope, which is not Christ. Bear witness to the goodness of Jesus in your online life, not simply your pet theological or political projects. Treat others with respect and kindness. Who you are online is who you are. You do not get a pass on biblical qualifications of gentleness and against quarrelsomeness simply because your venom is being mediated through a screen.

Obeying the command for pastors to be good citizens is an important way they may adorn the gospel with their lives, in effect making it look true. And living in a lost world as if the good news is *true* news is an important facet of gospel-driven ministry.

## Learning to Enjoy the Gospel

I have become convicted lately about the way I am prone to talk about pastoral ministry. I think, in a lot of ways, what the gospel-centered movement has given us in terms of the recovery of a more biblical ministry is a good corrective to the professionalization of the pastorate and a turning away from the therapeutic influence on religion. But I fear that too many of us have swung too far in another direction. I fear that I have swung too far in the other direction. I fear that for all my concern about making sure congregations know that their pastors carry heavy burdens and that they ought to be cared for deeply, that because I desire to ensure pastors know that their task is special and weighty and serious, and that in seeking to do justice to the grave realities of pastoral ministry, I have drifted too much into a mode of self-pity.

It's possible, I think, that we dwell too much on the bitter and not the sweet, the disgrace and not the honor, the sorrow and not the joy. But Jesus really did say that he came to make our joy complete! And he did not say "except for pastors." No matter the ministerial trials or congregational strife you have to endure, joy can be a dominant experience in your ministry.

Now, normal pastors get sad about sad things. Biblical joy is not about "putting on a happy face." But the fruit of our mystical connection with Christ through faith becoming our foundation is not the fruit of misery but of settled, persevering, all-flavoring *joy*. This joy is a disposition that says, "Life may stink, but eternal life is something to be seriously giddy about." There are at least three kinds of joy to be found in the work of pastoral ministry.

## Resting in God's Sovereignty over Your Ministry

Christ is the vine and the Father is the gardener (John 15:1). This really puts us in our place, doesn't it? What are you? A branch. Do you give life? No. The vine does that. Do you control growth? No. The gardener does that. What do you do? Make sure you stay connected to the vine.

I have not come across a doctrine so steadying for life and ministry than that of the absolute sovereignty of God over all things. I understand why this idea irritates so many people because it used to irritate me quite a bit. And I can't speak for anyone else, but what finally helped me turn the corner was realizing how idiotic it is to prefer a sense of *my* being in control rather than the Creator God of the universe, who is not just all-powerful but who loves me. He actually loves me more than I love me—at least as real love is counted.

The reality of the sovereignty of God over your ministry is the wellspring of a joyful rest, even as you're faithfully working hard to do everything he's commanded you. It makes so much of our ministry anxiety and control issues seem really, really pathetic.

Jesus says, "If you remain in me and my words remain in you, ask whatever you wish, and it will be done for you" (John 15:7). There is a wrong way to take this text. You could take it the way of the prosperity gospel and turn Jesus into a vending machine. But you know that's not what he means. The context bears out that Jesus is referring to fruitfulness. The "whatever you want" is not about health and wealth—not even ministerially—but is inextricably connected to the glory of the Father: "By this my Father is glorified, that you bear much fruit and so prove to be my disciples" (15:8 ESV). In other words, when you are so aligned with Christ, when you have lined up your "whatever you want" with the sovereign "whatever he wants," the fruit is guaranteed.

The Lord will be faithful to ensure the expansion of *his* name but not necessarily yours. The Lord may not share your dream for your ministry success. But he will bear fruit through your faithfulness.

And he will guarantee that when all is said and done, you will not regret the simple ministry of ordinary faith. So we find our joy not in success but in Christ. And we don't rejoice that our names are written in the *Who's Who of Pastoral Ministry* but in the Lamb's book of life!

## Knowing That Normal Ministry Will Produce Fruit

Ministerial fruitfulness can't always be about external measurements and growth; otherwise, many biblical scenarios don't make sense at all. Numeric, financial, and cultural growth isn't always the kind of fruitfulness the Scriptures hold out as the produce of the Spirit's work. In fact, many times the dynamic is such that outwardly, things look bleak, and yet inwardly, there is a great renewal of trust in God. "So we do not lose heart. Though our outer self is wasting away, our inner self is being renewed day by day" (2 Cor 4:16 ESV).

We also see this reflected in Galatians 5:16–24, where Paul provides a list of fleshly sins—bad things we do—and then contrasts that not with good things to do but with good things to be. A person can "act right" and not have a heart for God at all. Similarly, a church can look fruitful by worldly standards—numbers, dollars, influence—and not be advancing Christ's kingdom at all.

One of the scariest passages I ever encountered as a pastor was Ezekiel 37, where the Lord shows the prophet the valley of dry bones. There is a point in that vision where the bones begin to stir. But they do not have any breath in them. In other words, there's a very real possibility of something looking alive but actually being dead. Put that together with Revelation 3:1—"You have a reputation of being alive, but you are dead"—and it's a sobering reminder that sometimes a church can look successful but actually be spiritually dead, not bearing fruit that remains at all but only gathering sticks upon sticks to be burnt up on the last day.

By contrast, you may be struggling along, stretching every penny, pleading with gracious passion for repentance and belief while not seeing many or any conversions and still be fruitful in the ways that count eternally. In fact, Christ has guaranteed it. Big church or small church, successful pastor or struggling pastor, your fruitfulness is not contingent on your resources but on your Redeemer!

In fact, it is impossible to be united to Christ by faith and not bear fruit: "The one who remains in me and I in him produces much fruit, because you can do nothing without me. . . . My Father is glorified by this: that you produce much fruit and prove to be my disciples" (John 15:5b, 8 CSB). It's possible, pastor, that you are only planting the trees whose shade future pastors and churches will enjoy. The point is that every work done in faith for the glory of Christ will produce the fruit Christ has ordained and is pleased by.

There is no joy in trying to "produce" for Jesus. He's the one who produces. You can do nothing without him. This is so liberating. There is joy in knowing that normal ministry will produce fruit.

## Knowing Christ and Being His Friend

I do not mind continuing to beat this drum because it is the most important point communicated in this book. Above all the practical counsel, above all the congregational insight, above all the theological explanation, the most important thing I want pastors of churches to know is that they get to be friends with God.

> No one has greater love than this: to lay down his life for his friends. You are my friends if you do what I command you. I do not call you servants anymore, because a servant doesn't know what his master is doing. I have called you friends, because I have made known to you everything I have heard from my Father. (John 15:13–15 CSB)

Yes, you serve him, but not to earn his pleasure. He already delights in you. He already rejoices over you. His smile is already upon you. Christ has measured up on your behalf. Christ has made the sacrifice required for you to be square with God, so there's no need to keep paying down a debt with your ministry. The debt has been paid. You are not earning your keep!

Beat this into your own head continually. The burden of pastoral ministry ought to drive us constantly into the position of recentering on the gospel every day. Rehearsing our conversion. Reconverting, as it were, every day. There is so much joy to be had in the simple privilege of knowing Jesus and being his friend.

## For Reflection

1. How can you discern when to tell your wife sensitive information regarding church business and when it would be more appropriate to keep things confidential?
2. How can you plan your week in such a way that you can build and maintain a good reputation with outsiders?
3. What are some potential difficulties in maintaining close friendships with members of your congregation?
4. Do you struggle to engage in personal evangelism? Why or why not?
5. What does friendship with Jesus look like for you? How do you daily cultivate your relationship with him?

## For Further Study:

Cooley, Timothy Mather. *Sketches of the Life and Character of the Reverend Lemuel Haynes.* New York: Harper, 1837.

This biography of Haynes, the first African American pastor of an all-white congregation (Vermont, late eighteenth and early nineteenth centuries), was published shortly after Haynes's death but is still available in reprints and electronic editions. It is worth the read not just as an important historical

study of an oft-neglected portion of American church history
but as a revealing and edifying study of a pastor devoted
amply to his family and his wider community.

Edwards, Jonathan. *Heaven: A World of Love.* Carlisle, PA: Banner
of Truth, 2015.

This sermon from Edwards is readily available online
but also published in book form individually and in collected
works. Few short works can stir the heart to enjoy the gospel
more than this wondrous plunge into "the fountain of love."

Willard, Dallas. *The Divine Conspiracy: Rediscovering Our Hidden
Life in God.* New York: Harper, 1998.

The aim of the Christian life is discipleship of
Christ, becoming more like him every day through close
apprenticeship and friendship with him. Willard's book is
thick with wisdom toward this end, and it is a challenging
resource for embracing the gospel of the kingdom in your
everyday life.

# CHAPTER 10

# DYING

As I was nearing completion of the manuscript for this book, I thought I had a heart attack. It was a Saturday afternoon, and I was about forty-five minutes from preaching the closing session of the seminary's annual student conference. My text was Jude 24–25, the doxology. I was excited—maybe *too* excited!—but I felt very calm. I was sitting at my desk in my office and scrolling through my phone while listening to the preaching from the session before mine on the conference livestream. And suddenly something felt very wrong.

My heart rate began to surge. I could feel the beating in my chest. At the same time, I had the overwhelming sensation of my body "shutting down." It is still difficult to describe. I felt internally as though I was seizing up and was about to die. Beginning to panic, I decided I needed to exit my office and enter a public area where I might get help. Sitting down on a couch in the foyer, I signaled the seminary security that I was in distress. The officer who came to check on me was actually one of my ministry residents at the church. My situation worsened, and growing concerned, he called 911.

The EMTs arrived, stretcher in tow, and I made a fine sight sitting meekly on a couch as the conference broke and the lobby filled with a thousand teenagers, all seemingly gawking at my old-manness made humiliatingly manifest before them. I opted not to go to the hospital. My wife came to get me and took me home.

The next day we went to see the doctor. Blood was drawn. My heart was scanned. My personal and family history was scoured. It was determined I had not suffered a heart attack. However, my CardioScan showed a level of calcification in my heart that put me at intermediate risk of an attack. "At this rate," the doctor said, "you will have a heart attack in ten to twenty years."

"Oh, is that all?" I said. I actually wanted to know if it was more like eleven years or more like nineteen.

The diagnosis? An anxiety-induced panic attack. This was not a total surprise to me—remember those flashes of panic I mentioned in chapter 8?—but it was certainly a new development. I'd never suffered an attack outside of a driving situation. And it didn't feel quite the same. It felt more severe. In the six or seven years I have experienced sporadic trouble driving, I've never felt I needed emergency services or thought I was about to die. Now I've learned that these things have been building, and it can strike at any time.

Part of me wished the doctors had found something else. Something they could go in and take out. Something they could "clean up" or fix. Instead I have . . . anxiety. Even when I don't feel particularly nervous about anything.

"What were you doing when it happened?" people keep asking.

"Nothing," I say. "Just sitting there."

"Were you nervous about speaking?"

"No."

"Were you agitated about something?"

"No. I was literally just sitting at my desk, killing time until it was my turn to preach."

While I formulate a plan to manage this in the future—a stricter diet, more vigorous exercise, and, worst of all, cutting out caffeine—I have to reckon with the reality that my body is, as they say, "keeping the score." It feels like I have this ticking time bomb under my skin that can go off at any time without warning. A ghost haunting me. (Those of you who struggle with anxiety or depression or other mental health issues know what I mean.) I'm glad my condition isn't an imminent threat to my life, but I also have a daily reminder that this body is not how it was designed to be, that it is passing away. I am in fact dying. And you are too.

The week after all my doctor visits, while I was wrestling with this renewed reminder of my own frailty, the world mourned the loss of NBA star Kobe Bryant. For sports fans of a particular generation, he instantly became their most significant public loss. A sign that they are getting old, too. But Kobe wasn't old. Death does not discriminate. The same week, more sobering for me, was learning a pastor friend of mine had died of a heart attack. He was my age. He was in great shape, a CrossFitting bodybuilder and martial arts enthusiast. His heart just gave out.

A few weeks later, the world began to brace for the unknown impact of the COVID-19 pandemic, which at this writing has now persisted for months. Deaths are accumulating around the world. Economies are teetering. People are becoming more fearful, more anxious, more angry. Violent crime in our major cities has been increasing, along with the suicide rate everywhere.

This is the sting of life in a broken, sin-cursed world. Therefore, it is the mandate of every pastor to become well acquainted with death. And the truth is, there are a million little deaths to die along the road to the big one. Every day as we tend to Christ's flock, we are dealing, whether we realize it or not, with the necessity of our own death to self and the dying of self to others. I used to think that pastoral ministry was about helping people live. Then I learned it was actually about helping people die. These daily deaths, these momentary self-crucifixions, are in fact necessary for anyone who wants to live forever. "Die before you die," C. S. Lewis writes. "There is no chance after."[1]

Whether you are facing the daunting prospect of congregational conflict or your eyes are wide in wonder at seeing your "wish-dream" come to life, you must heed your death in Christ. Milton Vincent writes:

> When my flesh yearns for some prohibited thing, I must die. When called to do something I don't want to do, I must die. When I wish to be selfish and serve no one, I must die. When shattered by hardships that I despise, I must die. When wanting to cling to wrongs done against me, I must die. When enticed by allurements of the world, I must die. When wishing to keep besetting sins secret, I must die. When wants that are borderline needs are left unmet, I must die. When dreams that are good seem shoved aside, I must die.[2]

Do you die, pastor? Because you will. This will be your legacy, in fact—your demonstrating of life in Christ, having taken up his cross and having gloried in his resurrection. Everything else is shifting sand.

Shortly after I left the pastorate and moved to a new city to embark on a new season of ministry, I began visiting a Christian counselor, mainly to just process the mess of me. As I began to recount for him the weight of my previous ministry, how I had spent the last few years of my last assignment daily facing the darkness of death, the floodgates opened. I buried too many friends. Precious saints. Those with whom I'd eaten, laughed, cried, sung, and served. I walked with them all through weeks and months of suffering, seeing them across their finish line into glory. It seemed as though as soon as we'd put one in the ground, another one would become sick.

---

1. C. S. Lewis, *Till We Have Faces* (New York: Harcourt, 1957), 279.
2. Milton Vincent, *A Gospel Primer for Christians: Learning to See the Glories of God's Love* (Bemidji, MN: Focus, 2008), 41.

I was still mourning up until my final months of ministry. And at the same time, as I was caring at the bedside of a good friend who was dying of pancreatic cancer, I could sense some in the church turning on me. I endeavored to ignore the pain of that, to stuff it down deep within me. While I was helping someone die, the church was helping me die to self. And it was painful in ways I didn't recognize.

The counselor suggested I had never really processed all that death. I sort of laughed that off at the time. Now I think he was more right than either of us knew. I had come to him still licking some wounds from church life. I still carry the scars and calluses. I often lament them. But I also treasure them.

Paul contemplates his death this way:

> For I am already being poured out as a drink offering, and the time of my departure has come. I have fought the good fight, I have finished the race, I have kept the faith. Henceforth there is laid up for me the crown of righteousness, which the Lord, the righteous judge, will award to me on that day, and not only to me but also to all who have loved his appearing. (2 Tim 4:6–8 ESV)

Whatever pain or grief you are enduring (or will endure) in your ministry, picture getting to the end, whenever that may be, and feeling the rough places on your flesh, the fatigue in your bones, the weariness behind your eyes, and considering it all glory, all worth it, all part of the treasure of knowing Jesus and helping others know him too. I want to be known for my writing and preaching. But I hope my legacy is helping people see Jesus as they die.

I get asked this question a lot these days: "Do you miss pastoring?" The truth is, for the time being, I do not. I do sleep a lot better, for one thing! But the Lord has been sweet to confirm that I really did hear his voice in transitioning out. I know that the roles I serve in now, in the seminary and in public ministry and in contributing to my local church training future pastors, are right where God wants me. But part of the reason I don't miss it, honestly, is those scars. I don't feel the itch to jump back in (yet), but for the most part, it's because I am still tired of the suffering.

That friend I had the honor to last help finish well was named Natalie. When she got sick and began to need constant care, they set up hospice care in the basement apartment of her best friend, Ellen's, home. It was there that she died. It was there that we placed her in the plain pine box she'd designed herself for the occasion. It was there that my fellow elders and I, Natalie's husband Jim and Ellen's husband Dan at the head, prayed over her and shouldered the weight of her fragile body together. I remember the last time I drove down the winding gravel road away from Dan and Ellen's home after Natalie's passing.

A month later, I had resigned my post and moved away. A few years after that, Ellen got sick. Cancer again. I happened to be traveling in the area on a study tour and got in touch with Dan. I have to tell you, I was more than ready to take a sabbatical from helping people die. Dan asked if I would come visit. Honestly, I must confess I felt like the Michael Corleone line from *The Godfather, Part III* described my position perfectly: "Every time I think I'm out, they pull me back in." But I made the drive over, making my way slowly up that winding gravel road. A lot of feelings were rushing over me. It was all coming back.

She did not look good. She was practically skeletal. Lying on the couch, a pale version of her former feisty self, she smiled as I came near to hold her hand. At Dan's request, I shared the gospel with their daughters. We caught up on life and made conversation for a long while. Then I prayed with Ellen, a very long prayer, begging God to show the kindness he was (and is always) already eager to give. I gave Dan a tearful hug, and then I left and made that long drive back down the gravel road.

And do you know what? You know what I felt as I drove away? I felt inexplicably happy. Can you believe that? Does it seem weird? It occurred to me again in that moment that it is an overwhelming, mysterious *joy* to tend to Christ's lambs.

"And after you have suffered a little while, the God of all grace, who has called you to his eternal glory in Christ, will himself restore, confirm, strengthen, and establish you. To him be the dominion forever and ever. Amen" (1 Peter 5:10–11 ESV).

## For Reflection

1. When all is said and done, what do you want your "pastoral legacy" to be?
2. In what way(s) is "dying" the normal course of pastoral ministry?
3. What does helping people die look like for the gospel-centered pastor?
4. Describe a time in your life of difficulty or even suffering. What did God teach you about himself—and yourself—in those moments?
5. What are some gospel promises related to the prospect of death?

## For Further Study:

Baxter, Richard. *Dying Thoughts.* Carlisle, PA: Banner of Truth, 2004.

This meditation on Baxter's own fears and doubts—and a theological appraisal of them—is a valuable devotional read for any pastor interested in coming to gracious terms with his own mortality.

Lewis, C. S. *A Grief Observed.* New York: HarperOne, 1961.

Compiled from Lewis's private diaries of bereavement after the passing of his wife Joy, this book has comforted thousands upon thousands today with its poignant insights into the transience of life and the power of grace.

Owen, John. *The Mortification of Sin.* Abridged version. Carlisle, PA: Banner of Truth, 2004.

"Be killing sin or sin will be killing you." That is the driving force behind Owen's classic work, which is still the best guide to dying before you die.

Wells, John D. *The Pastor in the Sick Room: Ministering the Gospel to Those on the Brink of Eternity.* Port St. Lucie, FL: Solid Ground, 2004.

Helping people die is a nonnegotiable for gospel-driven pastoral ministry, and this short resource assembled from three Princeton Seminary addresses delivered by an early nineteenth century Presbyterian minister offers encouraging instruction for that work. It is both theological and practical.

# ON THE READINESS TO PASTOR

They didn't teach me this in seminary!" Whole books have been written addressing the alleged deficiencies of seminary education for the "real stuff" of pastoral ministry. It is quite common to hear ministers lamenting how ill-prepared they felt by their formal education for the rigors of pasture work.

I was never able to make this complaint. I did not receive a seminary degree until I'd conducted nearly twenty-five years of local church ministry without one. I didn't know exactly what *wasn't* taught in seminary during my pastorates, so I never thought to complain about it. Nevertheless, I think the complaint overwrought.

They can tell you about all kinds of things in seminary that only the experience of going through them can *actually teach* you. When I began my ministry to the local church, I was fully aware of the reality that people get sick and die. But no amount of foreknowledge could really prepare me for the sight, the sound, and even the smell of one of Christ's beloved lambs on the verge of death.

Not all seminaries and divinity schools are created equal, of course, but even the best theological education cannot prepare a minister for the experiential wisdom of *actually pastoring*. Now, serving at one of these institutions in the specific preparation of young men for pastoral ministry, I can tell you that we are unable to do what is beyond our purpose and ability. No academic training can. Even if the most ministerially astute student received the highest marks in achieving his Master of Divinity, these achievements in themselves would not make him ready to pastor.

As I tell my ministry students, if you read the assigned texts closely, take good notes from the lectures, and ask good questions in class, you can get a good grade. But if you don't take to heart what you're learning, cultivating through it an affection for God and for the church, it will be a waste. We're not making widgets. We're training ministers.

Even if we were to cover in class the reality of power-hungry deacons, deathbed counseling sessions, or bloated membership rolls—and we do—it would not prepare each student for the hundred different contextual and circumstantial factors that make these realities more complex in the field than they are on a page or whiteboard. When you're looking across the table or the hospital bed into real eyes, you can and should bring your education to mind, but you best bring your soul to bear.

So how do you know when you are ready? The truth is, *you are never ready when you start.* When you are about to assume your first pastorate, it does not matter how old you are, how much education you have, whether you have read all the right books, listened to all the right podcasts, read all the right blogs, attended all the right conferences, argued all the right doctrines, or whether you have your license or your ordination—you are not ready.

And here is why: Because you do not yet know whom you are pastoring. Now, you might know the name of the place and some names of the people in the place, but you do not yet know whom you are pastoring. You do not yet know whom you are loving.

There is nothing wrong with any of the training or accomplishments listed, and you should pursue all of them if you are able; but you are not ready to shepherd until you are neck deep with the sheep. You are not ready until you know what it is that keeps your people up at night, what it is, specifically, that breaks their hearts, what they are chasing after, what their hopes are, what their dreams are, what drives them during the day, what they are praying about, what they are worrying about, what they're worshiping when it's not God. You are not ready to shepherd until you have, in some way, had your heart moved by *these people*. And you are not ready to shepherd until you have had your heart in some way broken by these people.

In a way, it is like marriage. I look at the whole idea of the wedding ceremony as two idiots standing up in front of a group of people making all sorts of crazy promises. They are each assuming the best of each other as they say, "I am going to love you and forgive you, no matter what." Yet, they have no clue what that "no matter what" will be. The worst they can imagine is not that bad. Or at least they think they will be prepared when that time comes. But in the moment they make the promise, even though they do not know the cost, it is still a good thing. They should get married. They are ready to make the commitment. But until they have had their dreams of marriage shattered by their actual marriage, they will not know what the deal actually is.

The same is true for pastoral ministry. The shattering is the preparing. Getting filled up is a kind of preparation. But you're not ready until you've been broken open.

Previously, we saw how Paul instructs the church to meditate on their utter neediness:

Brothers and sisters, consider your calling: Not many were wise from a human perspective, not many powerful, not many of noble birth. Instead, God has chosen what is foolish in the world to shame the wise, and God has chosen what is weak in the world to shame the strong. God has chosen what is insignificant and despised in the world—what is viewed as nothing—to bring to nothing what is viewed as something, so that no one may boast in his presence. It is from him that you are in Christ Jesus, who became wisdom from God for us—our righteousness, sanctification, and redemption—in order that, as it is written: Let the one who boasts, boast in the Lord.

When I came to you, brothers and sisters, announcing the mystery of God to you, I did not come with brilliance of speech or wisdom. I decided to know nothing among you except Jesus Christ and him crucified. I came to you in weakness, in fear, and in much trembling. My speech and my preaching were not with persuasive words of wisdom but with a demonstration of the Spirit's power, so that your faith might not be based on human wisdom but on God's power. (1 Cor 1:26–2:5 CSB)

When we have been taken apart, we get to see how precious the grace of God is for binding up our wounds, reestablishing our feet, and announcing our place in the light of God's favor. The gospel is predicated on our frailty and spiritual inability.

A pastoral candidate who has not had a profound experience of the gospel is not ready. You are not ready to shepherd until you have been spiritually discombobulated by the gospel and essentially reconstituted by the gospel. I do not simply mean that you must have become a Christian. Of course you had better be a Christian! Pastors should be genuinely regenerated followers of Jesus. And I am not saying necessarily that you should not go ahead and become a pastor. I am just saying that until the gospel has undone you, until it has made you cry out, "Woe is me!" from your knees, you are not ready.

When you have tasted and seen that the Lord is good and it has ruined you for everything else, you are ready. When you have been hijacked by grace, you are ready. By his grace, then, brothers, you are ready to pastor when weakness and fear and trembling actually make sense to you.

That is ultimately what this book is about—navigating all the practical stuff of pastoral ministry in the light of heaven's unwieldy glory. Christian ministry is not built on religious know-how or leadership strategies. Christian ministry is the overflow of the mystery of God in Christ coming to bear on your soul and, through yours, on the souls of others. Pastoral ministry is the intentional and careful stewardship of the mystery of the gospel. When you feel intimidated by that reality, you might be ready.

# CONTEMPORARY READINGS
# FOR FURTHER STUDY

## The Pastor

Allen, Jason K. *Discerning Your Call to Ministry: How to Know for Sure and What to Do about It.* Chicago: Moody Publishers, 2016.

Charles, H. B., Jr. *On Pastoring: A Short Guide to Living, Leading, and Ministering as a Pastor.* Chicago: Moody Publishers, 2016.

Harvey, Dave. *Am I Called? The Summons to Pastoral Ministry.* Wheaton, IL: Crossway, 2012.

Rinne, Jeramie. *Church Elders: How to Shepherd God's People like Jesus.* Wheaton, IL: Crossway, 2014.

Strauch, Alexander. *Biblical Eldership: An Urgent Call to Restore Biblical Church Leadership.* Littleton, CO: Lewis and Roth, 1995.

Thune, Robert H. *Gospel Eldership: Equipping a New Generation of Servant Leaders.* Greensboro, NC: New Growth, 2016.

Wilson, Jared C. *The Pastor's Justification: Applying the Work of Christ in Your Life and Ministry.* Wheaton, IL: Crossway, 2013.

## The Power

Chandler, Matt, with Jared Wilson. *The Explicit Gospel.* Wheaton, IL: Crossway, 2012.

Gilbert, Greg. *What Is the Gospel?* Wheaton, IL: Crossway, 2010.

Keller, Timothy. *Center Church: Doing Balanced, Gospel-Centered Ministry in Your City.* Grand Rapids: Zondervan, 2012.

Ortlund, Ray. *The Gospel: How the Church Portrays the Beauty of Christ.* Wheaton, IL: Crossway, 2014.

Wilson, Jared C. *Gospel Wakefulness.* Wheaton, IL: Crossway, 2011.

## Worshiping

Bridges, Jerry, and Bob Bevington. *The Bookends of the Christian Life.* Wheaton, IL: Crossway, 2009.

Croft, Brian, and Jim Savastio. *The Pastor's Soul: The Call and Care of an Undershepherd.* Darlington, CO: Evangelical, 2018.

Dodson, Jonathan K. *Gospel-Centered Discipleship.* Wheaton, IL: Crossway, 2012.

Miller, Paul E. *A Praying Life: Connecting with God in a Distracting World.* Colorado Springs: NavPress, 2009.

## Preaching

Chapell, Bryan. *Christ-Centered Preaching: Redeeming the Expository Sermon.* 3rd ed. Grand Rapids: Baker Academic, 2018.

Charles, H. B., Jr. *On Preaching: Personal & Pastoral Insights for the Preparation & Practice of Preaching.* Chicago: Moody Publishers, 2014.

Eswine, Zack. *Preaching to a Post-Everything World: Crafting Biblical Sermons That Connect with Our Culture.* Grand Rapids: Baker, 2008.

Helm, David. *Expositional Preaching: How We Speak God's Word Today.* Wheaton, IL: Crossway, 2014.

Keller, Timothy. *Preaching: Communicating Faith in an Age of Skepticism.* New York: Viking, 2015.

Piper, John. *Expository Exultation: Christian Preaching as Worship.* Wheaton, IL: Crossway, 2018.

Smith, Robert, Jr. *Doctrine That Dances: Bringing Doctrinal Preaching and Teaching to Life.* Nashville: B&H Academic, 2008.

Wax, Trevin. *Gospel-Centered Teaching: Showing Christ in All the Scripture.* Nashville: B&H Academic, 2013.

## Caring

Eclov, Lee. *Pastoral Graces: Reflections on the Care of Souls*. Chicago: Moody Publishers, 2012.

Fernando, Ajith. *Jesus Driven Ministry*. Wheaton, IL: Crossway, 2002.

Furman, Dave. *Being There: How to Love Those Who Are Hurting*. Wheaton, IL: Crossway, 2016.

Kellemen, Robert W. *Gospel-Centered Counseling: How Christ Changes Lives*. Grand Rapids: Zondervan, 2014.

Senkbeil, Harold L. *The Care of Souls: Cultivating a Pastor's Heart*. Bellingham, WA: Lexham, 2019.

## Leading

Ayers, Mike. *Power to Lead: Five Essentials for the Practice of Biblical Leadership*. 2nd ed. Spring, TX: RBK, 2018.

Carson, D. A. *The Cross and Christian Ministry: Leadership Lessons from 1 Corinthians*. Grand Rapids: Baker, 1993.

Geiger, Eric, and Kevin Peck. *Designed to Lead: The Church and Leadership Development*. Nashville: B&H, 2016.

Sanchez, Juan. *The Leadership Formula: Develop the Next Generation of Leaders in the Church*. Nashville: B&H, 2020.

Thomas, Scott, and Tom Wood. *Gospel Coach: Shepherding Leaders to Glorify God*. Grand Rapids: Zondervan, 2012.

Wilson, Jared C. *The Gospel-Driven Church: Uniting Church Growth Dreams with the Metrics of Grace*. Grand Rapids: Zondervan, 2019.

## Fighting (and Making Peace)

Croft, Brian, and James B. Carroll. *Facing Snarls and Scowls: Preaching through Hostility, Apathy, and Adversity in Church Revitalization*. Fearn, Scotland: Christian Focus, 2019.

Heffelfinger, Curtis. *The Peacemaking Church: 8 Biblical Keys to Resolve Conflict and Preserve Unity*. Grand Rapids: Baker, 2018.

Leeman, Jonathan. *The Church and the Surprising Offense of God's Love: Reintroducing the Doctrines of Church Membership and Discipline*. Wheaton, IL: Crossway, 2010.

Poirier, Alfred. *The Peacemaking Pastor: A Biblical Guide to Resolving Church Conflict*. Grand Rapids: Baker, 2006.

Strauch, Alexander. *If You Bite and Devour One Another: Biblical Principles for Handling Conflict.* Littleton, CO: Lewis and Roth, 2011.

## Living

Croft, Brian and Cara. *The Pastor's Family: Shepherding Your Family through the Challenges of Pastoral Ministry.* Grand Rapids: Zondervan, 2013.

Eswine, Zack. *The Imperfect Pastor: Discovering Joy in Our Limitations through a Daily Apprenticeship with Jesus.* Wheaton, IL: Crossway, 2015.

Ortlund, Dane C. *Gentle and Lowly: The Heart of Christ for Sinners and Sufferers.* Wheaton, IL: Crossway, 2020.

Packer, J. I. *Weakness Is the Way: Life with Christ Our Strength.* Wheaton, IL: Crossway, 2018.

Scazzero, Peter. *The Emotionally Healthy Leader: How Transforming Your Inner Life Will Deeply Transform Your Church, Team, and the World.* Grand Rapids: Zondervan, 2015.

Wilson, Jared C. *Supernatural Power for Everyday People: Experiencing God's Extraordinary Spirit in Your Ordinary Life.* Nashville: Nelson, 2018.

## Dying

Alcorn, Randy. *Heaven.* Carol Stream, IL: Tyndale House, 2004.

McCullough, Matthew. *Remember Death: The Surprising Path to Living Hope.* Wheaton, IL: Crossway, 2018.

Prime, Derek. *A Good Old Age: An A to Z of Loving and Following the Lord Jesus in Later Years.* Leyland, UK: 10Publishing, 2017.

Tripp, Paul David. *Suffering: Gospel Hope When Life Doesn't Make Sense.* Wheaton, IL: Crossway, 2018.

Vroegop, Mark. *Dark Clouds, Deep Mercy: Discovering the Grace of Lament.* Wheaton, IL: Crossway, 2019.

# ACKNOWLEDGMENTS

This book is the product of more than twenty-five years of local church ministry, the last decade of which was supplemented with public ministry in consulting with and preaching in churches and ministry organizations around the world. Any wisdom you find within these pages is the fruit of the Lord's kindness and the direct result of being taught, encouraged, and otherwise influenced by countless ministers and other leaders who have been exceedingly generous to me.

I have to thank three pastors who have mentored me in critical moments in my life: Chris Trent, Mike Ayers, and Ray Ortlund.

I love pastors, and the pastoral fraternity, while a motley crew, is a precious one. I am grateful for these pastor friends who have encouraged me more than they know throughout the years: Caleb Brasher, David McLemore, Chris Lewis, Matt Chandler, Matt Capps, Josh Hedger, Ronni Kurtz, Chris Thomas, Phil Thomas, Steve Jeffrey, Roland Mitcheson, John Onwuchekwa, Won Kwak, Joe Thorn, Steve Bezner, Clint Pressley, Scott Harrison, Lucas Parks, Miles Rohde, Tim Kirkegard, Scotty Smith, Zack Eswine, Jonathan Leeman, and many more, whom space does not permit me to name. I love you all.

The ministry of Nathan Rose and his fellow elders at Liberty Baptist has been life-giving to my family.

Midwestern Seminary is a generous place to serve, and they have given me a wide ministry lane to run in and abundant freedom to write.

The residents, past and present, of the Pastoral Training Center at Liberty Baptist have kept me feeling useful.

The indefatigable work of agent par excellence Don Gates is beyond what I deserve, and I have been extraordinarily blessed by my Zondervan editor Ryan Pazdur, who patiently waited for this manuscript for too long.

Becky, Macy, and Grace have been the best partners in ministry a husband and father could have.